GRANDMA'S FAVORITES

TASTE OF HOME BOOKS • RDA ENTHUSIAST BRANDS, LLC • MILWAUKEE, WI

© 2020 RDA Enthusiast Brands, LLC.
1610 N. 2nd St., Suite 102, Milwaukee, WI 53212-3906
All rights reserved. Taste of Home is a registered trademark
of RDA Enthusiast Brands, LLC.

Visit us at tasteofhome.com for other
Taste of Home books and products.

ISBN: 978-1-61765-907-2
Component Number: 116700093H
LOCC: 2019949964

Executive Editor: Mark Hagen
Senior Art Director: Raeann Thompson
Assistant Art Director: Courtney Lovetere
Designer: Arielle Jardine
Copy Editor: Ann Walter

Cover:
Photographer: Mark Derse
Set Stylist: Melissa Franco
Food Stylist: Shannon Norris

Pictured on front cover:
Lemon Layer Cake, p. 98

Pictured on title page:
Great-Grandma's Oatmeal Cookies, p.89

Pattern:
Eva Marina/Shutterstock

Pictured on back cover:
Warm Fava Bean & Pea Salad, p. 79;
Traditional Meat Loaf, p. 71;
Yogurt Yeast Rolls, p. 29

Printed in USA
1 3 5 7 9 10 8 6 4 2

When you think of finger-licking, stick-to-your-ribs all-time comfort foods, Grandma's house quickly comes to mind. From the aroma of freshly baked breads to the satisfaction of a bubbling casserole and the anticipation of a down-home dessert, Grandma's kitchen never disappoints.

Relish these much-loved specialties in your home when you explore the 133 recipes in *Grandma's Favorites.* With these savory and sweet dishes, you'll delight in forgotten foods, add heartwarming flair to weeknight suppers and bring Grandma's special touch to holidays and other celebrations.

You'll also enjoy...

Grandma's Favorite Breakfasts. Remember sleepovers at Grandma's? The best food was always waiting first thing in the morning. Relive those moments with this eye-opening chapter of sunny classics.

Grandma's Favorite Main Courses. You can't go wrong when your meal features potpie, golden chicken or from-scratch spaghetti sauce. Don't forget hearty roasts, tasty lasagna and fish that's fried to perfection in a cast-iron skillet.

Grandma's Favorite Sunday Dinners. Surprise everyone at the table when you serve one of these complete menus inspired by Sunday meals with Grandma. The planning is done—let a deliciously delightful night begin!

Grandma's Favorite Desserts. Cakes and cobblers, tarts and tortes—here you'll find all the sweets you crave, as well as crispy cookies, decadent brownies and many other much-loved treats.

Relive those glorious moments around the table, create new memories in your kitchen and savor the goodness of the home-cooked foods you have always adored. It's easier than ever with this all-new keepsake, *Taste of Home Grandma's Favorites.*

CONTENTS

More ways to connect with us:

SHOPTASTEOFHOME.COM

BREAKFASTS

Whether made for a weekend sleepover or holiday brunch, Grandma's eye-opening breakfasts continuously warm hearts and satisfy tummies. Enjoy those sunny dishes once again with this collection of all-time classics.

BLUEBERRY CRUNCH BREAKFAST BAKE

BACON & ASPARAGUS FRITTATA

This quick and easy breakfast always wins me compliments with guests. It also makes a nice light dinner, especially in the summer, alongside servings of rice and bread.
—Gwen Clemon, Soldier, IA

- -

Prep: 10 min. • **Cook:** 25 min.
Makes: 6 servings

- 12 oz. bacon
- 2 cups sliced fresh asparagus (cut in ½-in. pieces)
- 1 cup chopped onion
- 2 garlic cloves, minced
- 10 large eggs, beaten
- ¼ cup minced parsley
- ½ tsp. seasoned salt
- ¼ tsp. pepper
- 1 large tomato, thinly sliced
- 1 cup shredded cheddar cheese

1. In a 9- or 10-in. ovenproof skillet, cook bacon until crisp. Drain, reserving 1 Tbsp. drippings. Heat the reserved drippings on medium-high. Add asparagus, onion and garlic; saute until onion is tender. Crumble bacon; set aside one third. In a large bowl, combine remaining bacon, eggs, parsley, salt and pepper.
2. Pour the egg mixture into the skillet; stir. Top with tomato, cheese and the reserved bacon. Cover and cook over medium-low until the eggs are nearly set, 10-15 minutes. Preheat broiler; place skillet 6 in. from heat. Broil until lightly browned, about 2 minutes. Serve immediately.
1 piece: 344 cal., 24g fat (10g sat. fat), 351mg chol., 738mg sod., 7g carb. (3g sugars, 2g fiber), 23g pro.

TEST KITCHEN TIP
Feeding a crowd? You can make this in a 12-in. skillet by increasing each ingredient by 50 percent and baking it for 20-25 minutes.

BLUEBERRY CRUNCH BREAKFAST BAKE

Blueberries in season make this delightful breakfast extra special, but I've discovered that frozen berries work just as well. My grandmother used to make this dish with strawberries, and I always looked forward to enjoying it at her house.
—Marsha Ketaner, Henderson, NV

- -

Prep: 15 min. • **Bake:** 30 min.
Makes: 12 servings

- 1 loaf (16 oz.) day-old French bread, cut into 1-in. slices
- 8 large eggs
- 1 cup half-and-half cream
- ½ tsp. vanilla extract
- 1 cup old-fashioned oats
- 1 cup packed brown sugar
- ¼ cup all-purpose flour
- ½ cup cold butter
- 2 cups fresh or frozen blueberries
- 1 cup chopped walnuts

1. Arrange half of the French bread slices in a greased 13x9-in. baking dish. Preheat oven to 375°.
2. In a large bowl, whisk the eggs, cream and vanilla. Slowly pour half of the cream mixture over the bread. Top with remaining bread and egg mixture. Let stand until the liquid is absorbed, about 5 minutes.
3. Meanwhile, in a small bowl, combine the oats, brown sugar and flour; cut in butter until crumbly. Sprinkle over top. Top with blueberries and walnuts.
4. Bake, uncovered, until a knife inserted in the center comes out clean, 30-35 minutes. Let stand for 5 minutes before serving.
1 serving: 427 cal., 21g fat (8g sat. fat), 154mg chol., 351mg sod., 50g carb. (23g sugars, 3g fiber), 12g pro.

BACON & ASPARAGUS FRITTATA

RASPBERRY BRAID

We like using blackberries, marionberries, a mixture of raspberries and blackberries or all three in this delicious, fast-to-fix pastry.
—Tressa Nicholls, Sandy, OR

- -

Prep: 20 min. • **Bake:** 15 min.
Makes: 12 servings

- 2 cups biscuit/baking mix
- 3 oz. cream cheese, cubed
- ¼ cup cold butter, cubed
- ⅓ cup 2% milk
- 1¼ cups fresh raspberries
- 3 Tbsp. sugar
- ¼ cup vanilla frosting

1. Preheat oven to 425°. Place the biscuit mix in a large bowl. Cut in cream cheese and butter until mixture resembles coarse crumbs. Stir in milk just until moistened. Turn dough onto a lightly floured surface; knead gently 8-10 times.
2. On a greased baking sheet, roll dough into an 18x12-in. rectangle. Spoon raspberries down the center third of dough; sprinkle with sugar.
3. On each long side, cut 1-in.-wide strips about 2½ in. into center. Starting at 1 end, fold alternating strips at an angle across raspberries; seal ends.
4. Bake until golden brown, 15-20 minutes. Remove to a wire rack to cool slightly. In a microwave-safe dish, microwave frosting on high until it reaches a desired consistency, 5-10 seconds; drizzle over pastry.
1 slice: 185 cal., 10g fat (5g sat. fat), 19mg chol., 319mg sod., 22g carb. (8g sugars, 1g fiber), 2g pro.

MUSHROOM & SMOKED SALMON TARTS

MUSHROOM & SMOKED SALMON TARTS

These yummy tarts came from a "what's-in-the-fridge?" moment, and they make a perfect dish for brunch or appetizers.
—Jacquelyn Benson, South Berwick, ME

- -

Prep: 30 min. + chilling • **Bake:** 15 min.
Makes: 2 tarts (6 servings each)

- 2 sheets refrigerated pie crust
- 1 Tbsp. olive oil
- 1 medium red onion, thinly sliced
- 1 Tbsp. butter
- 4 cups sliced fresh mushrooms (about 10 oz.)
- ⅔ cup smoked salmon or lox
- ⅓ cup crumbled feta cheese
- 8 large eggs, divided use
- 4 tsp. drained capers, divided
- ½ tsp. salt, divided
- ½ tsp. pepper, divided
- 2 tsp. snipped fresh dill, optional, divided

1. Unroll the crusts into two 9-in. fluted tart pans with removable bottoms; trim the edges. Refrigerate 30 minutes. Preheat oven to 400°.

2. Line the unpricked crusts with a double thickness of foil. Fill with pie weights, dried beans or uncooked rice. Bake on a lower oven rack until edges are golden brown, 10-15 minutes. Remove foil and weights; bake until the bottom is golden brown, 2-4 minutes longer. Cool on a wire rack. Reduce oven setting to 375°.
3. In a large skillet, heat oil over medium-high heat. Add onion; cook and stir until tender and lightly browned, 5-7 minutes. Remove from pan. Add butter and mushrooms; cook and stir 6-8 minutes or until mushrooms are tender. Cool slightly.
4. Place tart pans on separate baking sheets. Divide the onion and mushrooms between crusts; top with the salmon and feta cheese. In a bowl, whisk 4 eggs, 2 tsp. capers and ¼ tsp. each salt and pepper; if desired, stir in 1 tsp. dill. Pour over one of the tarts. Repeat with remaining ingredients for second tart.
5. Bake until a knife inserted in the center comes out clean, 15-20 minutes. Let stand 5 minutes before cutting.
1 piece: 239 cal., 15g fat (6g sat. fat), 136mg chol., 382mg sod., 18g carb. (2g sugars, 1g fiber), 8g pro.

BLUEBERRY-ORANGE BLINTZES

Blintzes are aces for morning meals because I can make the crepes ahead. They taste so indulgent that guests never guess they're lower in fat and calories!
—Mary Johnson, Coloma, WI

Prep: 15 min. + chilling • **Bake:** 25 min.
Makes: 6 servings

- 1 large egg
- 1 cup fat-free milk
- ¾ cup all-purpose flour
- 1 carton (15 oz.) part-skim ricotta cheese
- 6 Tbsp. orange marmalade, divided
- 1 Tbsp. sugar
- ⅛ tsp. ground cinnamon
- 2 cups fresh blueberries or raspberries, divided
- ⅔ cup reduced-fat sour cream

1. In a large bowl, whisk egg, milk and flour until blended. Refrigerate, covered, 1 hour.
2. Preheat oven to 350°. Place a 6-in. skillet coated with cooking spray over medium heat. Stir batter; fill a ¼-cup measure halfway with batter and pour into center of pan. Quickly lift and tilt pan to coat bottom evenly. Cook until top appears dry; turn crepe over and cook 15-20 seconds longer or until bottom is cooked. Remove to a wire rack. Repeat with remaining batter.
3. In a small bowl, mix the ricotta cheese, 2 Tbsp. marmalade, sugar and cinnamon. Spoon about 2 Tbsp. mixture onto each crepe; top with about 1 Tbsp. blueberries. Fold opposite sides of crepes over filling, forming a rectangular bundle.
4. Place blintzes on a 15x10x1-in. baking pan coated with cooking spray, seam side down. Bake, uncovered, 10-15 minutes or until heated through. Serve with sour cream and the remaining marmalade and blueberries.
Freeze option: Freeze the cooled crepes between layers of waxed paper in a freezer container. To use, thaw crepes overnight in refrigerator. Proceed as directed.
2 blintzes with toppings: 301 cal., 9g fat (5g sat. fat), 63mg chol., 129mg sod., 42g carb. (23g sugars, 2g fiber), 14g pro. **Diabetic exchanges:** 2 starch, 2 lean meat, ½ fruit.

GOLDEN OAT PANCAKES

My husband's face lights up when I make these country-style flapjacks. Serve them for a weekend breakfast or brunch, or you can freeze and heat them up later.
—Raymonde Bourgeois, Swastika, ON

Takes: 25 min. • **Makes:** 10 pancakes

- 1 cup old-fashioned oats
- 1⅓ cups 2% milk
- ¾ cup all-purpose flour
- 4 tsp. baking powder
- 4 tsp. brown sugar
- ¼ tsp. salt
- 2 large eggs, lightly beaten
- 3 Tbsp. canola oil

1. In a small bowl, mix oats and milk; let stand 5 minutes. In a large bowl, whisk flour, baking powder, brown sugar and salt.
2. Stir eggs and oil into oat mixture. Add to flour mixture; stir just until moistened.
3. Lightly grease a griddle; heat over medium heat. Pour batter by ¼ cupfuls onto griddle. Cook until bubbles on top begin to pop and bottoms are golden brown. Turn; cook until second side is golden brown.
Freeze option: Freeze the cooled pancakes between layers of waxed paper in a resealable freezer container. To use, place pancakes on an ungreased baking sheet, cover with foil and reheat in a preheated 375° oven 5-10 minutes. Or place 2 pancakes on a microwave-safe plate and microwave 1-1¼ minutes or until heated through.
2 pancakes: 270 cal., 13g fat (2g sat. fat), 80mg chol., 498mg sod., 30g carb. (7g sugars, 2g fiber), 8g pro.

BLUEBERRY-ORANGE BLINTZES

BUTTERMILK
WAFFLES

BUTTERMILK WAFFLES

You'll hear nothing but cheering from family and friends when you stack up these golden waffles for breakfast! My clan regularly requests this morning mainstay.
—Kim Branges, Grand Canyon, AZ

Takes: 25 min. • Makes: 16 (4-in.) waffles

- 1¾ cups all-purpose flour
- 1 tsp. baking powder
- 1 tsp. baking soda
- ½ tsp. salt
- 2 large eggs, room temperature
- 2 cups buttermilk
- ⅓ cup canola oil
  Optional: Sliced fresh strawberries, strawberry syrup and whipped cream

1. In a large bowl, combine the flour, baking powder, baking soda and salt. In another bowl, beat the eggs; add buttermilk and oil. Stir into dry ingredients just until combined.
2. Bake in a preheated waffle iron according to manufacturer's directions until golden brown. If desired, serve with sliced fresh strawberries, syrup and whipped cream.
2 waffles: 223 cal., 11g fat (2g sat. fat), 56mg chol., 435mg sod., 24g carb. (4g sugars, 1g fiber), 6g pro.

TOAD IN THE HOLE

This is one of the first recipes I taught my children to prepare when they were learning to cook. My little ones are now grown—and thankfully have advanced to more difficult recipes—but this continues to be a standby dish in my home and theirs.
—Ruth Lechleiter, Breckenridge, MN

Takes: 15 min. • Makes: 1 serving

- 1 slice of bread
- 1 tsp. butter
- 1 large egg
  Salt and pepper to taste

1. Cut a 3-in. hole in the middle of the bread and discard. In a small skillet, melt the butter; place the bread in the skillet.
2. Place egg in the hole. Cook for about 2 minutes over medium heat until the bread is lightly browned. Turn and cook the other side until egg yolk is almost set. Season with salt and pepper.
1 serving: 183 cal., 10g fat (4g sat. fat), 196mg chol., 244mg sod., 15g carb. (2g sugars, 1g fiber), 9g pro. Diabetic exchanges: 1 starch, 1 medium-fat meat, 1 fat.

HOMEMADE BISCUITS &
MAPLE SAUSAGE GRAVY

HOMEMADE BISCUITS & MAPLE SAUSAGE GRAVY

I remember digging into gravy-smothered, flaky biscuits on Christmas morning and other special occasions when I was a child. What a satisfying way to start the day!
—Jenn Tidwell, Fair Oaks, CA

Prep: 30 min. • Bake: 15 min.
Makes: 8 servings

- 2 cups all-purpose flour
- 3 tsp. baking powder
- 1 Tbsp. sugar
- 1 tsp. salt
- ¼ tsp. pepper, optional
- 3 Tbsp. cold butter, cubed
- 1 Tbsp. shortening
- ¾ cup 2% milk

SAUSAGE GRAVY
- 1 lb. bulk maple pork sausage
- ¼ cup all-purpose flour
- 3 cups 2% milk
- 2 Tbsp. maple syrup
- ½ tsp. salt
- ¼ tsp. ground sage
- ¼ tsp. coarsely ground pepper

1. Preheat oven to 400°. In a large bowl, whisk the flour, baking powder, sugar, salt and, if desired, pepper. Cut in butter and shortening until mixture resembles coarse crumbs. Add milk; stir just until moistened. Turn onto a lightly floured surface; knead gently 8-10 times.
2. Pat or roll dough to 1-in. thickness; cut with a floured 2-in. biscuit cutter. Place 1 in. apart on an ungreased baking sheet. Bake until golden brown, 15-17 minutes.
3. Meanwhile, in a large skillet, cook sausage over medium heat 6-8 minutes, breaking into crumbles, until no longer pink. Stir in flour until blended; gradually stir in milk. Bring to a boil, stirring constantly; cook and stir until sauce is thickened, 4-6 minutes. Stir in the remaining ingredients. Serve gravy with the warm biscuits.
1 biscuit with ½ cup gravy: 371 cal., 19g fat (8g sat. fat), 41mg chol., 915mg sod., 38g carb. (11g sugars, 1g fiber), 11g pro.

GRAN'S GRANOLA PARFAITS

When my mother-in-law has us come over for brunch, I particularly enjoy her parfaits. They are refreshing, light and wholesome. I made a few changes to her recipe and came up with this sweet, crunchy and nutty variation. Yum!

—Angela Keller, Newburgh, IN

- -

Prep: 15 min. • **Bake:** 30 min. + cooling
Makes: 16 servings

- 2 cups old-fashioned oats
- 1 cup Wheaties
- 1 cup whole almonds
- 1 cup pecan halves
- 1 cup sweetened shredded coconut
- 4½ tsp. toasted wheat germ
- 1 Tbsp. sesame seeds, toasted
- 1 tsp. ground cinnamon
- ¼ cup butter, melted
- 2 Tbsp. maple syrup
- 2 Tbsp. honey

- 1 can (20 oz.) pineapple tidbits, drained
- 1 can (15 oz.) mandarin oranges, drained
- 1 cup halved green grapes
- 2 to 3 medium firm bananas, sliced
- 1 cup sliced fresh strawberries
- 4 cups vanilla yogurt

1. Preheat oven to 350°. In a large bowl, combine first 8 ingredients. Combine butter, syrup and honey; drizzle over oat mixture and stir until well coated. Pour into a greased 13x9-in. baking pan. Bake, uncovered, for 30 minutes, stirring every 10 minutes. Cool on a wire rack; crumble granola into pieces.
2. Combine the fruits in a large bowl. For each parfait, layer 2 Tbsp. yogurt, 2 Tbsp. of granola and 3 rounded Tbsp. fruit in a parfait glass or dessert bowl. Repeat layers. Sprinkle with remaining granola. Serve immediately.
1 parfait: 327 cal., 17g fat (6g sat. fat), 13mg chol., 104mg sod., 39g carb. (26g sugars, 4g fiber), 8g pro.

OLD-WORLD PUFF PANCAKE

My grandmother taught my mom how to make this dish, which was popular during the Depression. During that time, cooks measured ingredients as pinches, dashes and dabs, but through the years accurate amounts have been noted. My wife and I continue to enjoy this treat today.

—Auton Miller, Piney Flats, TN

- -

Takes: 30 min. • **Makes:** 4 servings

- 2 Tbsp. butter
- 3 large eggs
- ¾ cup whole milk
- ¾ cup all-purpose flour
- 2 tsp. sugar
- 1 tsp. ground nutmeg
  Confectioners' sugar
  Lemon wedges
  Syrup, optional
  Fresh raspberries, optional

1. Preheat oven to 425°. Place butter in a 10-in. ovenproof skillet; place in oven until melted, 2-3 minutes. In a blender, process the eggs, milk, flour, sugar and nutmeg until smooth. Pour into prepared skillet.
2. Bake 16-18 minutes or until puffed and browned. Dust with confectioners' sugar. Serve with lemon wedges and, if desired, syrup and raspberries.
1 piece: 178 cal., 5g fat (2g sat. fat), 144mg chol., 74mg sod., 23g carb. (5g sugars, 1g fiber), 9g pro.

GRAN'S GRANOLA PARFAITS

MAPLE BACON WALNUT
COFFEE CAKE

CALICO SCRAMBLED EGGS

When you're short on time and scrambling to get a tasty meal on the table, this recipe is eggs-actly what you need. There's a short ingredient list, and cooking is kept to a minimum. Plus, with green pepper and tomato, it's colorful and fun.
—*Taste of Home* Test Kitchen

Takes: 15 min. • **Makes:** 4 servings

- 8 **large eggs**
- ¼ **cup 2% milk**
- ⅛ to ¼ tsp. **dill weed**
- ⅛ to ¼ tsp. **salt**
- ⅛ to ¼ tsp. **pepper**
- 1 Tbsp. **butter**
- ½ **cup chopped green pepper**
- ¼ **cup chopped onion**
- ½ **cup chopped fresh tomato**

1. In a bowl, whisk the first 5 ingredients until blended. In a 12-in. nonstick skillet, heat the butter over medium-high heat. Add green pepper and onion; cook and stir until tender. Remove from pan.
2. In same pan, pour in egg mixture; cook and stir over medium heat until eggs begin to thicken. Add tomato and pepper mixture; cook until heated through and no liquid egg remains, stirring gently.
1 cup: 188 cal., 13g fat (5g sat. fat), 381mg chol., 248mg sod., 4g carb. (3g sugars, 1g fiber), 14g pro. **Diabetic exchanges:** 2 medium-fat meat, ½ fat.

MAPLE BACON WALNUT COFFEE CAKE

The sleepyheads will roll out of bed right away when they smell this sweet and savory coffee cake baking! Nuts and bacon in the crumbly topping blend well with nutmeg, cinnamon and maple syrup.
—Angela Spengler, Niceville, FL

Prep: 25 min. • **Bake:** 35 min. + cooling
Makes: 24 servings

- 2½ cups **all-purpose flour**
- 1 cup **packed brown sugar**
- ½ tsp. **salt**
- ⅓ cup **cold butter**
- 2 tsp. **baking powder**
- ½ tsp. **baking soda**
- ½ tsp. **ground cinnamon**
- ¼ tsp. **ground nutmeg**
- 2 **large eggs, room temperature**
- 1½ cups **buttermilk**
- ½ cup **maple syrup**
- ⅓ cup **unsweetened applesauce**
- 5 **bacon strips, cooked and crumbled**
- ½ cup **chopped walnuts**

1. Preheat oven to 350°. In a large bowl, combine flour, brown sugar and salt. Cut in butter until crumbly. Set aside ½ cup for topping. Combine baking powder, baking soda, cinnamon and nutmeg; stir into the remaining flour mixture.
2. In a small bowl, whisk eggs, buttermilk, maple syrup and applesauce until well blended. Gradually stir into flour mixture until combined.
3. Spread into a 13x9-in. baking pan coated with cooking spray. Sprinkle with reserved topping, bacon and walnuts. Bake until a toothpick inserted in the center comes out clean, 35-40 minutes. Cool on a wire rack.
1 piece: 160 cal., 5g fat (2g sat. fat), 27mg chol., 183mg sod., 25g carb. (14g sugars, 1g fiber), 3g pro. **Diabetic exchanges:** 1½ starch, 1 fat.

GRANDMA'S FAVORITE
SNACKS

There are plenty of goodies, nibbles and bites at Grandma's house! Turn here when you need a tried-and-true snack or appetizer. From casual to formal, these party favorites make any get-together a bit more special.

CHICKEN FRIES

Kid-friendly and quick, these oven-baked bites are coated with a crunchy mixture of crushed potato chips, panko bread crumbs and Parmesan cheese. Dip them in ranch, barbecue sauce or honey mustard for an extra layer of irresistible flavor.
—Nick Iverson, Denver, CO

Prep: 20 min. • **Bake:** 15 min.
Makes: 4 servings

- 2 large eggs, lightly beaten
- ½ tsp. salt
- ½ tsp. garlic powder
- ¼ to ½ tsp. cayenne pepper
- 2 cups finely crushed ridged potato chips
- 1 cup panko (Japanese) bread crumbs
- ½ cup grated Parmesan cheese
- 2 boneless skinless chicken breasts (6 oz. each), cut into ¼-in.-thick strips

Preheat oven to 400°. In a shallow bowl, whisk eggs, salt, garlic powder and cayenne. In a separate shallow bowl, combine chips, bread crumbs and cheese. Dip chicken in egg mixture, then in potato chip mixture, patting to help coating adhere. Transfer to a greased wire rack in a foil-lined rimmed baking sheet. Bake until golden brown, 12-15 minutes.

1 serving: 376 cal., 17g fat (6g sat. fat), 149mg chol., 761mg sod., 27g carb. (1g sugars, 2g fiber), 27g pro.

CRABBIE PHYLLO CUPS

I always like to put a little extra chili sauce on top of these easy snacks. If you're out of crab, water-packed tuna works well, too.
—Johnna Johnson, Scottsdale, AZ

Takes: 20 min. • **Makes:** 2½ dozen

- ½ cup reduced-fat spreadable garden vegetable cream cheese
- ½ tsp. seafood seasoning
- ¾ cup lump crabmeat, drained
- 2 pkg. (1.9 oz. each) frozen miniature phyllo tart shells
- 5 Tbsp. chili sauce

In a small bowl, mix the cream cheese and seafood seasoning; gently stir in crab. Spoon 2 tsp. crab mixture into each tart shell; top with chili sauce.

1 filled phyllo cup: 34 cal., 2g fat (0 sat. fat), 5mg chol., 103mg sod., 3g carb. (1g sugars, 0 fiber), 1g pro.

BAKED CRAB DIP

BAKED CRAB DIP

We first enjoyed this exquisite crab dip at my grandson's wedding reception. Though it looks fancy, it's a snap to make. You can even fill the bread bowl early in the day and let it chill until serving. Just remove it from the refrigerator 30 minutes before baking.
—Marie Shelley, Exeter, MO

Prep: 15 min. • **Bake:** 45 min. • **Makes:** 5 cups

- 1 pkg. (8 oz.) cream cheese, softened
- 2 cups sour cream
- 2 cans (6 oz. each) crabmeat, drained, flaked and cartilage removed or 2 cups flaked imitation crabmeat
- 2 cups shredded cheddar cheese
- 4 green onions, thinly sliced
- 2 round loaves (1 lb. each) unsliced sourdough or Italian bread
  Additional sliced green onions, optional
  Assorted fresh vegetables, crackers

1. Preheat oven to 350°. In a bowl, beat the cream cheese until smooth. Add sour cream; mix well. Fold in crab, cheese and onions. Cut the top third off each loaf of bread; carefully hollow out the bottoms, leaving 1-in. shells. Cube the removed bread and tops; set aside. Spoon crab mixture into bread bowls. Place on baking sheets. Place the reserved bread cubes in a single layer around bread bowls.
2. Bake, uncovered, 45-50 minutes or until the dip is heated through. Garnish with green onions if desired. Serve with assorted fresh vegetables, crackers or toasted bread cubes.

2 Tbsp.: 100 cal., 6g fat (4g sat. fat), 24mg chol., 140mg sod., 7g carb. (1g sugars, 0 fiber), 4g pro.

GARDEN-FRESH SEAFOOD COCKTAIL

For something cool on a hot day, we like to mix shrimp and crab with crunchy veggies straight from the garden. Adobo seasoning adds the perfect hint of heat—look for it in your grocery's international section.
—Teri Rasey, Cadillac, MI

Prep: 15 min. + chilling • **Makes:** 6 cups

- ¾ lb. peeled and deveined cooked shrimp (31-40 per lb.), thawed
- 1 container (8 oz.) refrigerated jumbo lump crabmeat, drained
- 3 celery ribs, chopped
- 1 medium cucumber, peeled, seeded and chopped
- 1 medium sweet orange pepper, chopped
- 2 plum tomatoes, seeded and chopped
- ½ cup red onion, finely chopped
- 1 to 2 jalapeno peppers, seeded and finely chopped
- ¼ cup minced fresh cilantro
- 3 Tbsp. lime juice
- 1 Tbsp. olive oil
- 2¼ tsp. adobo seasoning

Combine first 9 ingredients. Whisk together lime juice, oil and adobo seasoning; drizzle over shrimp mixture and toss gently to coat. Refrigerate at least 1 hour, tossing gently every 20 minutes. Place shrimp mixture in cocktail glasses.

¾ cup: 103 cal., 3g fat (0 sat. fat), 92mg chol., 619mg sod., 5g carb. (2g sugars, 1g fiber), 15g pro.

CHEDDAR BACON BEER DIP

CHEDDAR BACON BEER DIP

This tangy, smoky dip won me the top prize at our office party recipe contest. You can use almost any beer—just steer clear of dark varieties.
—Ashley Lecker, Green Bay, WI

Takes: 25 min. • **Makes:** 4½ cups

- 18 oz. cream cheese, softened
- ¼ cup sour cream
- 1½ Tbsp. Dijon mustard
- 1 tsp. garlic powder
- 1 cup beer or nonalcoholic beer
- 1 lb. bacon strips, cooked and crumbled
- 2 cups shredded cheddar cheese
- ¼ cup heavy whipping cream
- 1 green onion, thinly sliced
  Soft pretzel bites

1. In a greased 6-qt. electric pressure cooker, combine cream cheese, sour cream, Dijon mustard and garlic powder until smooth. Stir in beer; add bacon, reserving 2 Tbsp. Lock the lid; close pressure-release valve. Adjust to pressure-cook on high for 5 minutes. Quick-release pressure.

2. Select the saute setting, and adjust for medium heat. Stir in the cheese and heavy cream. Cook and stir 3-4 minutes or until the mixture has thickened. Transfer to serving dish. Sprinkle with green onion and reserved bacon. Serve with soft pretzel bites.

¼ cup: 213 cal., 19g fat (10g sat. fat), 60mg chol., 378mg sod., 2g carb. (1g sugars, 0 fiber), 8g pro.

TEST KITCHEN TIP

To lighten up this popular dip, use reduced-fat cream cheese, light sour cream, half-and-half and reduced-fat shredded cheese. Serve with fresh celery and carrot sticks.

ASPARAGUS WRAPS

Asparagus makes a lovely finger food when it's wrapped in pastry with a cheesy, buttery filling. Serve this one to holiday guests, but keep it in mind for weeknight noshing, too!
—Linda Hall, Evington, VA

Prep: 20 min. • **Bake:** 15 min./batch
Makes: 2 dozen

- 3 Tbsp. butter, softened
- 1 Tbsp. Mrs. Dash Onion & Herb seasoning blend
- ¼ tsp. garlic salt
- 1 pkg. (17.3 oz.) frozen puff pastry, thawed
- 1 cup crumbled feta cheese
- 3 oz. thinly sliced prosciutto or deli ham
- 24 thick fresh asparagus spears, trimmed

1. Preheat oven to 425°. Mix softened butter, seasoning blend and garlic salt. Unfold puff pastry sheets onto a lightly floured surface. Spread each with 1½ Tbsp. butter mixture and sprinkle with ½ cup cheese. Top with the prosciutto, pressing lightly to adhere.
2. Using a pizza cutter or sharp knife, cut each sheet into 12 strips (about ½ in. thick). Wrap each strip, filling side in, around an asparagus spear; place on parchment-lined baking sheets.
3. Bake 15 minutes or until golden brown. Serve warm.
1 appetizer: 139 cal., 8g fat (3g sat. fat), 11mg chol., 248mg sod., 12g carb. (0 sugars, 2g fiber), 4g pro.

VANILLA ALMOND HOT COCOA

Show family and friends how much you love and appreciate them with this homemade cocoa. Its warm, rich flavor wards off even the coldest winter's chill!
—Vicki Holloway, Joelton, TN

Takes: 15 min. • **Makes:** 10 servings (2½ qt.)

- 1 cup sugar
- ⅔ cup baking cocoa
- ¼ tsp. salt
- 8 cups 2% milk
- ⅔ cup water
- 2 tsp. vanilla extract
- ½ tsp. almond extract
  Miniature marshmallows, optional

In a large saucepan, combine the sugar, cocoa and salt. Stir in milk and water. Cook and stir over medium heat until heated through. Remove from the heat; stir in extracts. Serve in mugs, with marshmallows if desired.
1 cup: 195 cal., 4g fat (2g sat. fat), 16mg chol., 151mg sod., 33g carb. (30g sugars, 1g fiber), 8g pro.

ASPARAGUS WRAPS

MARINATED MOZZARELLA

MAKE-AHEAD SAUSAGE PINWHEELS

Filled with sausage, sweet pepper and cream cheese, these roll-ups are excellent for unexpected visitors, a cocktail party or a halftime snack. Besides being easy to make, they can be done way ahead and kept in the freezer. All you have to do is pop them into a hot oven!
—Cindy Nerat, Menominee, MI

- -

Prep: 30 min. + freezing • **Bake:** 15 min.
Makes: about 6½ dozen

- 1 lb. bulk regular or spicy pork sausage
- ½ cup diced sweet red pepper
- 1 green onion, chopped
- 1 pkg. (8 oz.) cream cheese, cubed
- 2 tubes (8 oz. each) refrigerated crescent rolls

1. Preheat oven to 350°. In a large skillet, cook and crumble sausage over medium-high heat until no longer pink, 5-7 minutes; drain. Add pepper and green onion; cook and stir 2 minutes. Transfer to a bowl; cool 10 minutes. Stir in cream cheese until blended; cool completely.
2. Unroll one can of crescent dough and separate into four rectangles; pinch perforations to seal. Press each rectangle to 6x4½ in.; spread each with ⅓ cup filling to within ¼ in. of edges. Roll up jelly-roll style, starting with a short side; pinch seam to seal. Roll gently to make logs smooth. Place on a waxed paper-lined baking sheet, seam side down. Repeat with remaining crescent dough. Freeze, covered, until firm, about 1 hour.
3. Cut each log into 10 slices. Bake on parchment paper-lined baking sheets until golden brown, 15-18 minutes. Serve warm.
Freeze option: Freeze pinwheels in freezer containers, separating layers with waxed paper. To use, bake frozen pinwheels as directed, increasing time by 3-5 minutes.
1 appetizer: 46 cal., 3g fat (1g sat. fat), 6mg chol., 89mg sod., 2g carb. (1g sugars, 0 fiber), 1g pro.

MARINATED MOZZARELLA

I always come home with an empty container when I bring this dish to a party. It can be made ahead to free up time later. I serve it with pretty party picks for a festive look.
—Peggy Cairo, Kenosha, WI

- -

Prep: 15 min. + marinating
Makes: 10 servings

- ⅓ cup olive oil
- 1 Tbsp. chopped oil-packed sun-dried tomatoes
- 1 Tbsp. minced fresh parsley
- 1 tsp. crushed red pepper flakes
- 1 tsp. dried basil
- 1 tsp. minced chives
- ¼ tsp. garlic powder
- 1 lb. cubed part-skim mozzarella cheese

In a large bowl, combine first seven ingredients; add cheese cubes. Stir to coat. Cover; refrigerate at least 30 minutes.
¼ cup: 203 cal., 16g fat (7g sat. fat), 24mg chol., 242mg sod., 2g carb. (trace sugars, trace fiber), 12g pro.

LOADED BAKED POTATO DIP

I never thought of using waffle-cut fries as a scoop for dip until a friend of mine did at a baby shower. They're ideal for my cheesy bacon and chive dip, which tastes just like a baked potato topper.
—Elizabeth King, Duluth, MN

- -

Takes: 10 min.
Makes: 2½ cups (10 servings)

- 2 cups reduced-fat sour cream
- 2 cups shredded reduced-fat cheddar cheese
- 8 center-cut bacon or turkey bacon strips, chopped and cooked
- ⅓ cup minced fresh chives
- 2 tsp. Louisiana-style hot sauce
   Hot cooked waffle-cut fries

In a small bowl, mix the first five ingredients until blended; refrigerate until serving. Serve with waffle fries.
¼ cup: 149 cal., 10g fat (6g sat. fat), 38mg chol., 260mg sod., 4g carb. (4g sugars, 0 fiber), 11g pro.

MAKE-AHEAD
SAUSAGE
PINWHEELS

CRANBERRY MEATBALLS

Lots of people have asked me for this recipe, but I knew I had a real winner when even my grandmother asked me for it!
—Tammy Neubauer, Ida Grove, IA

Prep: 20 min. • **Bake:** 20 min.
Makes: 6 dozen

- 2 large eggs, lightly beaten
- 1 cup cornflake crumbs
- ⅓ cup ketchup
- 2 Tbsp. dried minced onion
- 2 Tbsp. soy sauce
- 1 Tbsp. dried parsley flakes
- ½ tsp. salt
- ¼ tsp. pepper
- 2 lbs. ground pork

SAUCE

- 1 can (14 oz.) jellied cranberry sauce
- 1 cup ketchup
- 3 Tbsp. brown sugar
- 1 Tbsp. lemon juice

1. Preheat oven to 350°. Mix the first 8 ingredients. Add pork; mix lightly but thoroughly. Shape into 1-in. meatballs. Place on a greased rack in a 15x10x1-in. pan. Bake 20-25 minutes or until a thermometer reads 160°. Drain meatballs on paper towels.
2. In a large skillet, cook and stir the sauce ingredients over medium heat until blended. Stir in meatballs; heat through.
1 meatball: 58 cal., 2g fat (1g sat. fat), 16mg chol., 142mg sod., 6g carb. (4g sugars, 0 fiber), 3g pro.

CHICKEN & BACON ROLL-UPS

My children like these so much that they ask for them every day for lunch in the summer. Whenever I have leftover chicken or turkey breast, this is a delicious way to use it up.
—Patricia Nieh, Portola Valley, CA

Prep: 20 min. + chilling • **Makes:** 4 dozen

- 1 can (9¾ oz.) chunk white chicken, drained
- 1 carton (8 oz.) spreadable garden vegetable cream cheese
- 1 cup salsa, divided
- 4 pieces ready-to-serve fully cooked bacon, crumbled
- 6 flour tortillas (8 in.), room temperature

Mix chicken, cream cheese, ½ cup salsa and bacon; spread over tortillas. Roll up tightly; wrap in plastic. Refrigerate at least 1 hour. Just before serving, unwrap and cut tortillas into 1-in. slices. Serve with remaining salsa.
1 roll-up: 43 cal., 2g fat (1g sat. fat), 4mg chol., 100mg sod., 4g carb. (0 sugars, 0 fiber), 3g pro.

CRANBERRY MEATBALLS

**DEEP-FRIED
MAC & CHEESE SHELLS**

CHEWY CARAMEL-
COATED POPCORN

When I was a kid, my mom often made this sweet snack. I've since adapted it to make a chewy, gooey version, and now I'm asked to make this regularly. Packed into decorative bags, it makes a welcome hostess gift.
—Shannon Dobos, Calgary, AB

- -

Takes: 25 min. • **Makes:** about 6 qt.

1½ cups butter, cubed
2⅔ cups packed light brown sugar
 1 cup golden syrup
 1 tsp. vanilla extract
24 cups popped popcorn

1. Line two 15x10x1-in. pans with parchment. In a large heavy saucepan, melt butter over medium-high heat. Add brown sugar and syrup, stirring to dissolve brown sugar. Bring to a full rolling boil. Boil and stir 1 minute. Remove from heat and quickly stir in vanilla.
2. Pour caramel mixture over popcorn; stir lightly to coat. Using a rubber spatula, press popcorn into prepared pans. Cool. Pull apart into pieces. Store in airtight containers.
Note: This recipe was tested with Lyle's Golden Syrup.
1 cup: 303 cal., 16g fat (8g sat. fat), 31mg chol., 216mg sod., 40g carb. (35g sugars, 1g fiber), 1g pro.

DEEP-FRIED
MAC & CHEESE SHELLS

I created this dish for my husband because mac and cheese is one of his favorites. He calls these shells "unbelievably delicious" because of their crispy coating and creamy richness on the inside.
—Shirley Rickis, Lady Lake, Fl

- -

Prep: 45 min. • **Cook:** 15 min.
Makes: 20 appetizers (2½ cups dipping sauce)

 2 cups uncooked small pasta shells
20 uncooked jumbo pasta shells
 2 Tbsp. butter
 1 pkg. (16 oz.) Velveeta, cubed
 2 cups shredded cheddar cheese
 1 cup heavy whipping cream
 ¾ cup grated Parmesan cheese, divided
1¼ cups 2% milk, divided
 2 large eggs
 2 cups panko (Japanese) bread crumbs
 ½ cup all-purpose flour
  Oil for deep-fat frying

1. Cook pastas separately according to the package directions for al dente; drain. Meanwhile, in a large saucepan, melt butter over low heat. Add the Velveeta, cheddar cheese, cream and ¼ cup Parmesan cheese. Cook and stir over low heat until blended. Remove from heat.
2. In another large saucepan, combine small pasta shells and half of the cheese mixture; set aside. For dipping sauce, stir 1 cup milk into remaining cheese mixture; keep warm.
3. In a shallow bowl, whisk eggs with the remaining milk. In another shallow bowl, mix bread crumbs with remaining Parmesan. Place flour in a third shallow bowl. Fill each large shell with scant ¼ cup pasta mixture. Dip in flour to coat all sides; shake off excess. Dip in egg mixture, then in bread crumb mixture, patting to help coating adhere.
4. In an electric skillet or deep fryer, heat oil to 375°. Fry shells, a few at a time, until dark golden brown, 1-2 minutes on each side. Drain on paper towels. Serve shells with dipping sauce.
1 appetizer with 2 Tbsp. dipping sauce: 340 cal., 23g fat (10g sat. fat), 72mg chol., 451mg sod., 21g carb. (3g sugars, 1g fiber), 12g pro.

GRANDMA'S FAVORITE

BREADS, BISCUITS & MORE

Dinner rolls and doughnuts, sweet muffins and herb loaves: Let the aroma of these freshly baked delights usher in heartwarming memories of Grandma's kitchen today.

GARDEN VEGETABLE CORNBREAD

HUNGARIAN NUT ROLLS

It's never officially Christmas until I've made this treasured recipe passed down from my husband's grandmother. The apple-walnut filling has the most amazing flavor.
—Donna Bardocz, Howell, MI

- -

Prep: 40 min. + rising
Bake: 30 min. + cooling
Makes: 4 loaves (12 slices each)

2	pkg. (¼ oz. each) active dry yeast
½	cup warm 2% milk (110° to 115°)
¼	cup plus 2 Tbsp. sugar
¾	tsp. salt
1	cup butter, softened
1	cup sour cream
3	large eggs, lightly beaten
6	to 6½ cups all-purpose flour

FILLING

1¼	cups sugar
½	cup butter, cubed
1	large egg
½	tsp. ground cinnamon
4½	cups ground walnuts
1	large apple, peeled and grated

ICING

2	cups confectioners' sugar
2	to 3 Tbsp. 2% milk

1. In a large bowl, dissolve yeast in warm milk. Add the sugar, salt, butter, sour cream, eggs and 3 cups of flour. Beat on medium speed until smooth, about 3 minutes. Stir in enough remaining flour to form a soft dough (dough will be sticky).
2. Turn onto a floured surface; knead until smooth and elastic, 6-8 minutes. Place in a greased bowl, turning once to grease top. Cover and let dough rise in a warm place until doubled, about 1 hour.
3. Meanwhile, in a large saucepan, combine the sugar, butter, egg and cinnamon. Cook and stir over medium heat until mixture is thick enough to coat the back of a spoon. Remove from the heat; gently stir in walnuts and apple. Cool completely.
4. Punch dough down. Turn onto a lightly floured surface; divide into 4 portions. Roll each into a 12x10-in. rectangle. Spread filling to within ½ in. of edges. Roll up jelly-roll style, starting with a long side; pinch seams to seal. Place seam side down on greased baking sheets. Cover rolls and let rise until doubled, about 30 minutes.
5. Bake at 350° for 30-40 minutes or until lightly browned. Remove from pans to wire racks to cool. Combine the icing ingredients; drizzle over loaves.

1 slice: 222 cal., 12g fat (5g sat. fat), 36mg chol., 87mg sod., 26g carb. (13g sugars, 1g fiber), 4g pro.

GARDEN VEGETABLE CORNBREAD

When I was a kid, my parents would always make cornbread for me and my siblings. We would slather butter and maple syrup over the warm bread, and it was delicious. Today, I experiment a lot with recipes, just like my grandma and mom did, and that's how this healthier version of their easy cornbread recipe was born!
—Kim Moyes, Kenosha, WI

- -

Prep: 20 min. • **Bake:** 20 min.
Makes: 9 servings

1	cup yellow cornmeal
¾	cup whole wheat flour
2½	tsp. baking powder
2	tsp. minced fresh chives
¾	tsp. salt
2	large eggs, room temperature
1	cup 2% milk
2	Tbsp. honey
¾	cup shredded carrots (about 1½ carrots)
¼	cup finely chopped sweet red pepper
¼	cup finely chopped fresh poblano pepper, seeded

1. Preheat oven to 400°. Whisk together first 5 ingredients. In another bowl, whisk eggs, milk and honey until blended. Add to cornmeal mixture; stir just until moistened. Fold in carrots and peppers.
2. Transfer to a greased 8-in. square baking pan. Bake until a toothpick inserted in the center comes out clean, 20-25 minutes. Serve warm.

1 piece: 149 cal., 2g fat (1g sat. fat), 44mg chol., 367mg sod., 28g carb. (6g sugars, 2g fiber), 5g pro. **Diabetic exchanges:** 2 starch.

HUNGARIAN NUT ROLLS

CELERY-ONION POPOVERS

I found the handwritten recipe for these in a cookbook I got from my mom. With onion and celery, these pleasing popovers taste a little like stuffing.
—Barbara Carlucci, Orange Park, FL

- -

Prep: 15 min. • **Bake:** 40 min.
Makes: 9 servings

2 cups all-purpose flour
1 tsp. onion salt
⅛ tsp. celery salt
4 large eggs, room temperature
2 cups whole milk
¼ cup grated onion
¼ cup grated celery
3 Tbsp. butter, melted

1. Preheat oven to 450°. In a large bowl, combine the flour, onion salt and celery salt. Combine the eggs, milk, onion, celery and butter; whisk into the dry ingredients just until blended. Grease and flour the bottom and sides of 9 popover cups; fill two-thirds full with batter.
2. Bake 15 minutes. Reduce heat to 350° (do not open oven door). Bake 25 minutes longer or until deep golden brown (do not underbake). Immediately cut a slit in the top of each popover to allow steam to escape.
1 popover: 202 cal., 8g fat (4g sat. fat), 98mg chol., 306mg sod., 25g carb. (3g sugars, 1g fiber), 7g pro.

OLD-WORLD
RYE BREAD

OLD-WORLD RYE BREAD

This traditional bread gets some of its flavor from rye and caraway, but it's baking cocoa that gives it a beautiful dark color in addition to its wonderful taste. For a fun variation, stir in a cup each of raisins and walnuts.
—Perlene Hoekema, Lynden, WA

- -

Prep: 25 min. + rising
Bake: 35 min. + cooling
Makes: 2 loaves (12 slices each)

2 pkg. (¼ oz. each) active dry yeast
1½ cups warm water (110° to 115°)
½ cup molasses
6 Tbsp. butter, softened
2 cups rye flour
¼ cup baking cocoa
2 Tbsp. caraway seeds
2 tsp. salt
3½ to 4 cups all-purpose flour
Cornmeal

1. In a large bowl, dissolve yeast in warm water. Beat in the molasses, butter, rye flour, baking cocoa, caraway seeds, salt and 2 cups all-purpose flour until smooth. Stir in enough of the remaining all-purpose flour to form a stiff dough.
2. Turn onto a floured surface; knead until smooth and elastic, for about 6-8 minutes. Place in a greased bowl, turning once to grease top. Cover and let dough rise in a warm place until doubled, about 1½ hours.
3. Punch dough down. Turn onto a lightly floured surface; divide in half. Shape each piece into a loaf, about 10 in. long. Grease 2 baking sheets; sprinkle with cornmeal. Place loaves on prepared pans. Cover and let rise until doubled, about 1 hour.
4. Bake at 350° for 35-40 minutes or until bread sounds hollow when tapped. Remove from pans to wire racks to cool.
1 slice: 146 cal., 3g fat (2g sat. fat), 8mg chol., 229mg sod., 26g carb. (5g sugars, 2g fiber), 3g pro.

YOGURT YEAST ROLLS

Bring these fluffy, golden rolls to a potluck and people will eat them up in a hurry! It's a nice contribution because rolls are easy to transport, and one batch goes a long way.
—Carol Forcum, Marion, IL

Prep: 30 min. + rising • **Bake:** 15 min.
Makes: 2 dozen

- 1½ cups whole wheat flour
- 3¼ cups all-purpose flour, divided
- 2 pkg. (¼ oz. each) active dry yeast
- 2 tsp. salt
- ½ tsp. baking soda
- 1½ cups plain yogurt
- ½ cup water
- 3 Tbsp. butter
- 2 Tbsp. honey
  Additional melted butter, optional

1. In a large bowl, combine whole wheat flour, ½ cup all-purpose flour, yeast, salt and baking soda. In a saucepan over low heat, heat yogurt, water, butter and honey to 120°-130°. Pour over dry ingredients; blend well. Beat on medium speed for 3 minutes. Add enough remaining all-purpose flour to form a soft dough.
2. Turn onto a floured surface; knead until smooth and elastic, about 6-8 minutes. Place in a greased bowl, turning once to grease top. Cover and let rise in a warm place until doubled, about 1 hour.
3. Punch dough down. Turn onto a lightly floured surface; divide into 24 portions. Roll each into a 10-in. rope. Shape rope into an "S," then coil each end until it touches the center. Place 3 in. apart on greased baking sheets. Cover rolls and let rise until doubled, about 30 minutes. Preheat oven to 400°.
4. Bake the rolls until golden brown, about 15 minutes. If desired, brush the tops with additional butter while warm. Remove from pans to wire racks to cool.
1 roll: 115 cal., 2g fat (1g sat. fat), 6mg chol., 245mg sod., 21g carb. (3g sugars, 1g fiber), 3g pro. **Diabetic exchanges:** 1½ starch, ½ fat.

DOUBLE CHOCOLATE BANANA MUFFINS

The yummy combination of two favorite flavors—chocolate and banana—makes these muffins doubly good.
—Donna Brockett, Kingfisher, OK

Prep: 15 min. • **Bake:** 20 min.
Makes: about 1 dozen

- 1½ cups all-purpose flour
- 1 cup sugar
- ¼ cup baking cocoa
- 1 tsp. baking soda
- ½ tsp. salt
- ¼ tsp. baking powder
- 1⅓ cups mashed ripe bananas (about 3 medium)
- ⅓ cup canola oil
- 1 large egg, room temperature
- 1 cup (6 oz.) miniature semisweet chocolate chips

1. Preheat oven to 350°. Whisk together the first 6 ingredients. In a separate bowl, whisk bananas, oil and egg until blended. Add to flour mixture; stir just until moistened. Fold in chocolate chips.
2. Fill greased or paper-lined muffin cups three-fourths full. Bake 20-25 minutes or until a toothpick inserted in center comes out clean. Cool 5 minutes before removing from pan to a wire rack. Serve warm.
1 muffin: 278 cal., 11g fat (3g sat. fat), 16mg chol., 220mg sod., 45g carb. (28g sugars, 2g fiber), 3g pro.

YOGURT YEAST ROLLS

BUTTERY HERB LOAVES

BUTTERY HERB LOAVES

This is one of my family's favorite breads. They especially love it served with a warm bowl of soup when there's a chill in the air.
—Lillian Hatcher, Plainfield, IL

Prep: 45 min. + rising
Bake: 20 min. + cooling
Makes: 2 loaves (16 slices each)

- 4 to 5 cups all-purpose flour
- 1 pkg. (¼ oz.) active dry yeast
- ¼ cup sugar
- 1 tsp. salt
- 1¼ cups 2% milk
- ⅓ cup butter, cubed
- 2 large eggs, room temperature

FILLING
- ½ cup butter, softened
- 1 garlic clove, minced
- ½ tsp. dried minced onion
- ½ tsp. dried basil
- ½ tsp. caraway seeds
- ¼ tsp. dried oregano
- ⅛ tsp. cayenne pepper

1. In a large bowl, combine 2 cups flour, yeast, sugar and salt. In a small saucepan, heat milk and butter to 120°-130°. Add to dry ingredients; beat just until moistened. Add eggs; beat until smooth. Stir in enough remaining flour to form a soft dough.
2. Turn onto a floured surface; knead until smooth and elastic, about 6-8 minutes. Place in a greased bowl, turning once to grease top. Cover and let rise in a warm place until doubled, about 1 hour.
3. In a small bowl, combine filling ingredients; set aside. Punch down dough; divide in half. Turn onto a lightly floured surface. Roll each portion into a 15x9-in. rectangle. Spread filling over each to within ½ in. of edges. Roll up jelly-roll style, starting with a short side; pinch seams to seal and tuck ends under.
4. Place seam side down in 2 greased 9x5-in. loaf pans. Cover and let rise in a warm place until doubled, about 30 minutes. Preheat the oven to 350°.
5. Bake 20-25 minutes or until golden brown. Cool for 10 minutes before removing from pans to wire racks to cool completely.
1 slice: 109 cal., 5g fat (3g sat. fat), 27mg chol., 116mg sod., 13g carb. (2g sugars, 0 fiber), 3g pro. **Diabetic exchanges:** 1 starch, 1 fat.

AMISH ONION CAKE

AMISH ONION CAKE

This rich, moist bread with an onion-poppy seed topping is a wonderful break from your everyday breads. You can serve it with any meat, and it's a nice accompaniment to soup or salad. I've made it many times and have often been asked to share the recipe.
—Mitzi Sentiff, Annapolis, MD

Prep: 25 min. • **Bake:** 35 min.
Makes: 12 servings

- 3 to 4 medium onions, chopped
- 2 cups cold butter, divided
- 1 Tbsp. poppy seeds
- 1½ tsp. salt
- 1½ tsp. paprika
- 1 tsp. coarsely ground pepper
- 4 cups all-purpose flour
- ½ cup cornstarch
- 1 Tbsp. baking powder
- 1 Tbsp. sugar
- 1 Tbsp. brown sugar
- 5 large eggs, room temperature
- ¾ cup 2% milk
- ¾ cup sour cream

1. In a large skillet, cook onions in ½ cup butter over low heat for 10 minutes. Stir in poppy seeds, salt, paprika and pepper; cook until the onions are golden brown, stirring occasionally. Remove from heat; set aside.
2. In a large bowl, combine flour, cornstarch, baking powder and sugars. Cut in 1¼ cups butter until the mixture resembles coarse crumbs. Melt the remaining butter. In a small bowl, whisk the eggs, milk, sour cream and melted butter. Make a well in dry ingredients; stir in egg mixture just until moistened.
3. Spread into a greased 10-in. cast-iron skillet or springform pan. Spoon the onion mixture over the batter. Place pan on a baking sheet. Bake at 350° until a toothpick inserted in the center comes out clean, for 35-40 minutes. Serve warm.
1 piece: 539 cal., 36g fat (22g sat. fat), 182mg chol., 748mg sod., 44g carb. (7g sugars, 2g fiber), 9g pro.

CARDAMOM BRAID BREAD

I came across this recipe in 1983, and I've been making it ever since. The braid might look complicated, but you can rest assured, the resulting baked beauty is so worth it!
—Rita Bergman, Olympia, WA

- -

Prep: 30 min. + rising
Bake: 20 min. + cooling
Makes: 2 loaves (20 slices each)

- 6 cups all-purpose flour
- 2 pkg. (¼ oz. each) active dry yeast
- 1½ tsp. ground cardamom
- 1 tsp. salt
- 1½ cups plus 2 Tbsp. 2% milk, divided
- ½ cup butter, cubed
- ½ cup honey
- 2 large eggs, room temperature
- 2 Tbsp. sugar

1. In a large bowl, combine 2 cups flour, yeast, cardamom and salt. In a small saucepan, heat 1½ cups milk, butter and honey to 120°-130°. Add to dry ingredients; beat just until moistened. Add eggs; beat until smooth. Stir in enough remaining flour to form a firm dough (dough will be sticky).
2. Turn onto a floured surface; knead until smooth and elastic, about 6-8 minutes. Place in a greased bowl, turning once to grease top. Cover and let rise in a warm place until doubled, about 45 minutes.
3. Punch dough down. Turn onto a lightly floured surface; divide in half. Divide each portion into thirds. Shape each into a 14-in. rope. Place 3 ropes on a greased baking sheet and braid; pinch ends to seal and tuck under. Repeat with remaining dough. Cover and let rise until doubled, about 30 minutes. Preheat oven to 375°.
4. Brush with remaining milk and sprinkle with sugar. Bake 20-25 minutes or until golden brown. Remove from pans to wire racks to cool.

1 slice: 114 cal., 3g fat (2g sat. fat), 18mg chol., 91mg sod., 19g carb. (5g sugars, 1g fiber), 3g pro.

TENDER WHOLE WHEAT ROLLS

Even though these rolls are whole wheat, they have a light, soft texture. They remind me of lots of happy meals with my family.
—Wilma Orlano, Carroll, IA

- -

Prep: 40 min. + rising • **Bake:** 10 min.
Makes: 2 dozen

- 1½ cups boiling water
- ⅓ cup wheat bran
- 3 Tbsp. ground flaxseed
- 1½ tsp. salt
- 1 tsp. ground cinnamon
- ⅓ cup honey
- ¼ cup canola oil
- 2 pkg. (¼ oz. each) active dry yeast
- ¼ cup warm water (110° to 115°)
- 2 tsp. sugar
- 1½ cups whole wheat flour
- 2½ to 3 cups bread flour

1. In a small bowl, pour boiling water over the wheat bran, flaxseed, salt and cinnamon. Add honey and oil. Let stand until mixture cools to 110°-115°, stirring occasionally.
2. In a large bowl, dissolve yeast in warm water. Add the sugar, whole wheat flour and wheat bran mixture. Beat on medium speed for 3 minutes. Stir in enough bread flour to form a firm dough.
3. Turn onto a floured surface; knead until smooth and elastic, about 6-8 minutes. Place in a greased bowl, turning once to grease the top. Cover and let rise in a warm place until doubled, about 1 hour. Punch dough down.
4. Turn onto a lightly floured surface; divide into 24 pieces. Shape each into a roll. Place 2 in. apart on greased baking sheets. Cover and let rise until doubled, about 30 minutes. Preheat oven to 375°.
5. Bake until golden brown, 10-15 minutes. Remove from pans to wire racks to cool.

1 roll: 120 cal., 3g fat (0 sat. fat), 0 chol., 149mg sod., 22g carb. (4g sugars, 2g fiber), 4g pro. **Diabetic exchanges:** 1½ starch, ½ fat.

TENDER WHOLE WHEAT ROLLS

APPLE CIDER DOUGHNUTS

NO-KNEAD KNOT ROLLS

When I was growing up on our Iowa farm, my mom loved to serve these light, golden rolls. They're easy since they don't require kneading, and the dough rises in the fridge overnight, so there's hardly any last-minute bother when you need fresh hot rolls to serve with your meal.
—Toni Hilscher, Omaha, NE

Prep: 25 min. + rising • **Bake:** 10 min.
Makes: 4 dozen

- 2 pkg. (¼ oz. each) active dry yeast
- 2 cups warm water (110° to 115°)
- ½ cup sugar
- 2 tsp. salt
- 6 to 6½ cups all-purpose flour
- 1 large egg, room temperature
- ½ cup shortening
- ½ cup butter, softened

1. In a large bowl, dissolve yeast in warm water. Add the sugar, salt and 2 cups flour. Beat on medium speed for 2 minutes. Beat in egg and shortening. Stir in enough remaining flour to form a soft dough (do not knead). Cover and refrigerate overnight.
2. Punch dough down; divide into 4 portions. Roll each portion into a 14x12-in. rectangle. Spread 2 Tbsp. butter over dough. Fold in half lengthwise; cut into 12 strips. Tie each strip into a knot; tuck and pinch ends under. Place 2 in. apart on greased baking sheets. Repeat with remaining dough.
3. Cover and let rise until doubled, about 1 hour. Bake at 400° until golden brown, 10-12 minutes. Remove to wire rack to cool.
1 roll: 102 cal., 4g fat (2g sat. fat), 10mg chol., 119mg sod., 14g carb. (2g sugars, 0 fiber), 2g pro.

APPLE CIDER DOUGHNUTS

When I was a kid, my family always stopped to pick up cake doughnuts like these before camping in the Badlands. Share a batch with someone you know who appreciates the old-fashioned taste of fresh doughnuts. Try the gingered sugar for extra goodness.
—Melissa Hansen, Ellison Bay, WI

Prep: 40 min. + chilling • **Cook:** 5 min./batch
Makes: 1 dozen doughnuts plus doughnut holes

- 2 cups apple cider
- 3 cups all-purpose flour
- ½ cup whole wheat flour
- ⅔ cup packed brown sugar
- 2 tsp. baking powder
- ¾ tsp. salt
- ½ tsp. baking soda
- ¼ tsp. each ground cardamom, nutmeg, cinnamon and allspice
- 2 large eggs, room temperature
- 6 Tbsp. butter, melted and cooled
  Oil for deep-fat frying
  Ginger-Sugar for topping, optional

1. In a small saucepan, bring cider to a rapid boil; cook over high heat until reduced by half, about 12 minutes. Cool completely.
2. Whisk together flours, brown sugar, baking powder, salt, baking soda and spices. In a separate bowl, whisk eggs, melted butter and cooled cider; stir into dry ingredients just until moistened (dough will be sticky). Refrigerate, covered, until firm enough to shape, about 1 hour.
3. Divide dough in half. On a floured surface, pat each portion to ½-in. thickness; cut with a floured 3-in. doughnut cutter.
4. In an electric skillet or deep fryer, heat oil to 325°. Fry doughnuts, a few at a time, until golden brown, 2-3 minutes on each side. Fry doughnut holes, a few at time, until golden brown and cooked through, about 1 minute on each side. Drain on paper towels; cool slightly. If desired, dip apple cider doughnuts into ginger-sugar.
1 serving: 335 cal., 15g fat (5g sat. fat), 46mg chol., 338mg sod., 45g carb. (16g sugars, 1g fiber), 5g pro.
Ginger-Sugar: In a shallow bowl, mix ¾ cup sugar and 2-3 Tbsp. ground ginger. Dip warm doughnuts in mixture to coat. **Makes:** ¾ cup.

GRANDMA'S FAVORITE
SOUPS & STEWS

All-time classics such as Grandma's chicken and dumplings and hearty beef stew deliver comforting goodness as few foods can. These satisfying dishes always guarantee a smile, so turn the page and ladle out a bit of love today.

GARLICKY CHEDDAR CHEESE BISQUE

I gave my traditional cheddar cheese soup a boost with a hearty yet healthy variety of root vegetables. Crushed pita chips and fresh parsley make fun garnishes.
—Patricia Harmon, Baden, PA

Prep: 30 min. • **Cook:** 40 min.
Makes: 6 servings (1½ qt.)

- 1 Tbsp. butter
- 1 Tbsp. canola oil
- 1 medium leek (white portion only), sliced
- ½ cup chopped carrot
- ½ cup chopped celery
- ½ cup chopped peeled parsnip
- 1 tsp. salt
- ½ tsp. pepper
- 6 garlic cloves, minced
- 2 cans (14½ oz. each) chicken broth
- ⅔ cup dry white wine
- 2 Tbsp. cornstarch
- ¼ cup cold water
- 1 can (12 oz.) evaporated milk
- 2 cups shredded sharp white cheddar cheese
  Crushed baked pita chips
  Minced fresh parsley

1. In a large saucepan, heat butter and oil over medium heat. Add vegetables, salt and pepper; cook and stir 7-8 minutes or until vegetables are crisp-tender. Add garlic; cook 1-2 minutes longer.

2. Stir in the broth and wine; bring to a boil. Reduce the heat; simmer, uncovered, for 15-20 minutes or until vegetables are tender. Remove from heat; cool slightly. Meanwhile, in a small bowl, mix the cornstarch and water until smooth.

3. Process the soup in batches in a food processor until smooth. Return all to pan. Stir in evaporated milk and cornstarch mixture; bring to a boil. Reduce the heat; simmer, uncovered, until thickened and bubbly, stirring frequently. Add cheese; cook and stir until cheese is blended. Top servings with crushed pita chips and parsley.

1 cup: 320 cal., 19g fat (12g sat. fat), 68mg chol., 1307mg sod., 18g carb. (9g sugars, 1g fiber), 13g pro.

FROGMORE STEW

This old-fashioned medley of shrimp, smoked kielbasa, corn and spuds is a specialty of South Carolina cuisine. It's commonly dubbed Frogmore stew or Beaufort stew in recognition of both of the low country communities that lay claim to its origin. No matter what you call it, this one-pot wonder won't disappoint!
—*Taste of Home* Test Kitchen

Prep: 10 min. • **Cook:** 35 min.
Makes: 8 servings

- 16 cups water
- 1 large sweet onion, quartered
- 3 Tbsp. seafood seasoning
- 2 medium lemons, halved, optional
- 1 lb. small red potatoes
- 1 lb. smoked kielbasa or fully cooked hot links, cut into 1-in. pieces
- 4 medium ears sweet corn, cut into thirds
- 2 lbs. uncooked medium shrimp, peeled and deveined
  Seafood cocktail sauce
  Melted butter
  Additional seafood seasoning

1. In a stockpot, combine water, onion, seafood seasoning and, if desired, lemons; bring to a boil. Add the red potatoes; cook, uncovered, 10 minutes. Add kielbasa and corn; return to a boil. Reduce heat; simmer, uncovered, 10-12 minutes or until potatoes are tender. Add shrimp; cook 2-3 minutes longer or until shrimp turn pink.

2. Drain; transfer to a bowl. Serve with cocktail sauce, butter and additional seasoning.

1 serving: 369 cal., 18g fat (6g sat. fat), 175mg chol., 751mg sod., 24g carb. (7g sugars, 2g fiber), 28g pro.

GARLICKY CHEDDAR CHEESE BISQUE

FROGMORE
STEW

EGG DROP SOUP

I found this recipe in my grandma's old cookbook, and we continue to start many stir-fry meals with it. The easy soup cooks in just minutes flat, and while there are many recipe variations, but we like the addition of cornstarch to thicken the soup and give it a rich, golden color.

—Amy Beth Corlew-Sherlock, Lapeer, MI

Takes: 15 min. • **Makes:** 4 servings

- 3 cups chicken broth
- 1 Tbsp. cornstarch
- 2 Tbsp. cold water
- 1 large egg, lightly beaten
- 1 green onion, sliced

1. In a large saucepan, bring broth to a boil over medium heat. Combine cornstarch and water until smooth; gradually stir into broth. Bring to a boil; cook and stir for 2 minutes or until thickened.
2. Reduce heat. Drizzle beaten egg into hot broth, stirring constantly. Remove from the heat; stir in onion.
¾ cup: 39 cal., 2g fat (0 sat. fat), 53mg chol., 714mg sod., 3g carb. (1g sugars, 0 fiber), 3g pro.

CARROT SOUP WITH ORANGE & TARRAGON

CARROT SOUP WITH ORANGE & TARRAGON

A pretty orange color, a delicious hint of citrus and a garden-fresh flavor make this soup a requested dish at celebrations. Try sprinkling individual bowls with fresh tarragon before serving.

—Phyllis Schmalz, Kansas City, KS

Prep: 20 min. • **Cook:** 20 min.
Makes: 8 servings (2 qt.)

- 2 lbs. fresh carrots, sliced
- 2 medium onions, chopped
- 2 Tbsp. butter
- 6 cups reduced-sodium chicken broth
- 1 cup orange juice
- 2 Tbsp. brandy
- 4 tsp. minced fresh tarragon or ½ tsp. dried tarragon
- 1 tsp. salt
- 1 tsp. pepper
- 8 tarragon sprigs

1. In a Dutch oven, saute carrots and onion in butter for 8-10 minutes or until onion is tender. Add the broth; bring to a boil. Reduce heat; simmer, uncovered, for 10-12 minutes or until carrots are very tender. Cool slightly.
2. In a blender, process soup in batches until smooth. Return all to pan; stir in the orange juice, brandy and minced tarragon. Bring to a boil. Reduce heat; simmer, uncovered, for 5 minutes to allow flavors to blend. Season with salt and pepper. Garnish with tarragon sprigs before serving.
1 cup: 117 cal., 3g fat (2g sat. fat), 8mg chol., 823mg sod., 18g carb. (10g sugars, 4g fiber), 4g pro.

STEPHANIE'S SLOW-COOKER STEW

Start this warming one-pot meal before you head out for the day. By the time you get home, the well-seasoned meat will be tender and mouthwatering.
—Stephanie Rabbitt-Schapp, Cincinnati, OH

Prep: 20 min. • **Cook:** 7½ hours
Makes: 5 servings (about 1½ qt.)

- 1 lb. beef stew meat
- 2 medium potatoes, peeled and cubed
- 1 can (14½ oz.) beef broth
- 1 can (11½ oz.) V8 juice
- 2 celery ribs, chopped
- 2 medium carrots, chopped
- 1 medium sweet onion, chopped
- 3 bay leaves
- ½ tsp. salt
- ½ tsp. dried thyme
- ½ tsp. chili powder
- ¼ tsp. pepper
- 2 Tbsp. cornstarch
- 1 Tbsp. cold water
- ½ cup frozen corn
- ½ cup frozen peas

1. In a 3-qt. slow cooker, combine the first 12 ingredients. Cover and cook on low for 7-8 hours or until meat is tender. Discard bay leaves.
2. In a small bowl, combine the cornstarch and water until smooth; stir into stew. Add corn and peas. Cover and cook on high until thickened, about 30 minutes.
1⅓ cups: 273 cal., 7g fat (2g sat. fat), 56mg chol., 865mg sod., 31g carb. (9g sugars, 4g fiber), 22g pro. **Diabetic exchanges:** 3 lean meat, 2 vegetable, 1 starch.

STEPHANIE'S SLOW-COOKER STEW

QUICK CHICKEN & DUMPLINGS

Oh, the things you can make with frozen biscuit dough. The biscuits give this classic dish a speedy makeover. I like to use the buttermilk variety.
—Lakeya Astwood, Schenectady, NY

Takes: 30 min. • **Makes:** 6 servings (2¼ qt.)

- 6 individually frozen biscuits
- ¼ cup chopped onion
- ¼ cup chopped green pepper
- 1 Tbsp. olive oil
- 4 cups shredded rotisserie chicken
- 3 cans (14½ oz. each) reduced-sodium chicken broth
- 1 can (4 oz.) mushroom stems and pieces, drained
- 1 tsp. chicken bouillon granules
- 1 tsp. minced fresh parsley
- ½ tsp. dried sage leaves
- ¼ tsp. dried rosemary, crushed
- ¼ tsp. pepper

1. Cut each biscuit into fourths; set aside. In a large saucepan, saute onion and green pepper in oil until tender. Stir in the chicken, broth, mushrooms, bouillon granules, parsley, sage, rosemary and pepper.
2. Bring to a boil. Reduce heat; add biscuits for dumplings. Cover and simmer until a toothpick inserted in the center of a dumpling comes out clean (do not lift the cover while simmering), about 10 minutes.
1½ cups: 420 cal., 20g fat (5g sat. fat), 83mg chol., 1443mg sod., 26g carb. (6g sugars, 1g fiber), 34g pro.

ROOT
VEGETABLE
BISQUE

ROOT VEGETABLE BISQUE

I like cozy comfort soups that taste creamy but without the cream. This one's full of good stuff like rutabagas, leeks, fresh herbs and almond milk.
—Merry Graham, Newhall, CA

- -

Prep: 25 min. • **Cook:** 50 min.
Makes: 12 servings (3 qt.)

- ¼ cup dairy-free spreadable margarine
- 2 tsp. minced fresh chives
- 2 tsp. minced fresh parsley
- ½ tsp. grated lemon zest
BISQUE
- 2 Tbsp. olive oil
- 2 large rutabagas, peeled and cubed (about 9 cups)
- 1 large celery root, peeled and cubed (about 3 cups)
- 3 medium leeks (white portion only), chopped (about 2 cups)
- 1 large carrot, cubed (about ⅔ cup)
- 3 garlic cloves, minced
- 7 cups vegetable stock
- 2 tsp. minced fresh thyme
- 1½ tsp. minced fresh rosemary
- 1 tsp. salt
- ½ tsp. coarsely ground pepper
- 2 cups almond milk
- 2 Tbsp. minced fresh chives

1. Mix first 4 ingredients. Using a melon baller or 1-tsp. measuring spoon, shape mixture into 12 balls. Freeze on a waxed paper-lined baking sheet until firm. Transfer herbed margarine balls to freezer container; freeze up to 2 months.
2. In a 6-qt. stock pot, heat oil over medium heat; saute rutabagas, celery root, leeks and carrot for 8 minutes. Add the garlic; cook and stir for 2 minutes. Stir in stock, herbs, salt and pepper; bring to a boil. Reduce the heat; simmer, covered, until vegetables are tender, 30-35 minutes.
3. Puree soup using an immersion blender, or cool slightly and puree in batches in a blender; return to pan. Stir in milk; heat through. Top servings with chives and herbed margarine.
1 cup: 146 cal., 7g fat (2g sat. fat), 0 chol., 672mg sod., 20g carb. (9g sugars, 5g fiber), 3g pro. **Diabetic exchanges:** 1 starch, 1 fat.

GRANDMA'S
PEA SOUP

GRANDMA'S PEA SOUP

My grandma's soup was a family favorite. What makes it different from any other pea soups I have tried is the addition of whole peas, spaetzle-like dumplings and sausage. Try it once and you'll be hooked.
—Carole Talcott, Dahinda, IL

- -

Prep: 15 min. + soaking • **Cook:** 2¾ hours
Makes: 16 servings (4 qt.)

- ½ lb. dried whole peas
- ½ lb. dried green split peas
- 1 meaty ham bone
- 3 qt. water
- 1 large onion, chopped
- 1 medium carrot, chopped
- 2 celery ribs, chopped
- ½ cup chopped celery leaves
- 1 tsp. bouquet garni (mixed herbs)
- 1 Tbsp. minced fresh parsley
- 1 bay leaf
- 1 tsp. salt
- ¼ tsp. pepper
- ½ lb. smoked sausage, chopped, optional

SPAETZLE DUMPLINGS
- 1 cup all-purpose flour
- 1 large egg, beaten
- ⅓ cup water

1. Cover peas with water and soak overnight. Drain, rinse and place in a Dutch oven.
2. Add ham bone, water and remaining soup ingredients except sausage and dumplings. Bring to a boil. Reduce heat; cover and simmer 2-2½ hours.
3. Remove ham bone and skim fat. Remove meat from bone; dice. Add the ham and, if desired, sausage to pan.
4. For dumplings, place flour in a small bowl. Make a depression in the center of the flour; add egg and water and stir until smooth.
5. Place a colander with ³⁄₁₆-in.-diameter holes over simmering soup; transfer dough to the colander and press through with a wooden spoon. Cook the soup, uncovered, for 10-15 minutes. Discard bay leaf.
Freeze option: Prepare soup without dumplings and freeze in serving-size portions to enjoy for months to come.
1 cup: 155 cal., 2g fat (1g sat. fat), 20mg chol., 171mg sod., 26g carb. (2g sugars, 6g fiber), 9g pro.

LEMONY TURKEY RICE SOUP

While growing up in Texas, I spent a lot of time helping my grandma cook. Lemon and cilantro add a deliciously different twist to our turkey soup.
—Margarita Cuellar, East Chicago, IN

Takes: 30 min. • **Makes:** 8 servings (2 qt.)

- 2 cups diced cooked turkey
- 2 cups cooked long grain rice
- 1 can (10¾ oz.) condensed cream of chicken soup, undiluted
- ¼ tsp. pepper
- 6 cups chicken broth, divided
- 2 Tbsp. cornstarch
- ¼ to ⅓ cup lemon juice
- ¼ to ½ cup minced fresh cilantro

1. In a saucepan, combine first 4 ingredients and 5½ cups broth. Bring to a boil; cook for 3 minutes.

2. In a small bowl, mix cornstarch and remaining broth until smooth; gradually stir into soup. Bring to a boil; cook and stir until thickened, 1-2 minutes. Remove from heat; stir in lemon juice and cilantro.
1 cup: 166 cal., 4g fat (1g sat. fat), 42mg chol., 1047mg sod., 17g carb. (1g sugars, 1g fiber), 13g pro.

> "I made this easy soup exactly according to the recipe, and it was very tasty! My friend and her mother were also fans. It's very comforting on a chilly evening, and I'll be making it again."
> —VETZLER, TASTEOFHOME.COM

PESTO BEAN SOUP

This is one of my all-time favorite vegetarian recipes. I make large batches on cold winter days, and I freeze the leftovers. Homemade pesto is tasty, but you can use store-bought to make the dish simple. Serve the soup with garlic toast and a green salad.
—Liz Bellville, Tonasket, WA

Prep: 10 min. • **Cook:** 4 hours
Makes: 8 servings (2½ qt.)

- 1 carton (32 oz.) reduced-sodium vegetable broth
- 1 large white onion, chopped
- 4 garlic cloves, minced
- 2½ cups sliced baby portobello mushrooms
- 3 cans (15 to 15½ oz. each) cannellini beans, rinsed and drained
- ¾ cup prepared pesto, divided
- ¼ cup grated Parmigiano Reggiano cheese

In a 4-qt. slow cooker, combine the first 5 ingredients. Stir in ½ cup pesto. Cook, covered, on low until vegetables are tender, 4-6 hours. Before serving, stir in reserved pesto and cheese. If desired, serve with additional cheese and pesto.
1¼ cups: 244 cal., 9g fat (2g sat. fat), 2mg chol., 586mg sod., 30g carb. (3g sugars, 8g fiber), 9g pro. **Diabetic exchanges:** 2 starch, 1½ fat, 1 lean meat.

LEMONY TURKEY RICE SOUP

BUTTERNUT SQUASH CHILI

BUTTERNUT SQUASH CHILI

Add butternut squash to chili for a tasty, filling, energy-packed dish that your whole family will love. Mine does!
—Jeanne Larson, Rancho Santa Margarita, CA

- -

Prep: 20 min. • **Cook:** 30 min.
Makes: 8 servings (2 qt.)

- 1 lb. ground beef or turkey
- ¾ cup chopped red onion
- 5 garlic cloves, minced
- 3 Tbsp. tomato paste
- 1 Tbsp. chili powder
- 1 tsp. ground cumin
- ½ to 1 tsp. salt
- 1¾ to 2 cups water
- 1 can (15 oz.) black beans, rinsed and drained
- 1 can (15 oz.) pinto beans, rinsed and drained
- 1 can (14½ oz.) diced tomatoes
- 1 can (14½ to 15 oz.) tomato sauce
- 3 cups cubed peeled butternut squash, (½-in. cubes)
- 2 Tbsp. cider vinegar
  Optional: Chopped avocado, plain Greek yogurt and shredded mozzarella cheese

1. In a Dutch oven over medium heat, cook beef and onion, crumbling meat, 6-8 minutes or until beef is no longer pink and the onion is tender.
2. Add next 5 ingredients; cook 1 minute longer. Stir in water, beans, diced tomatoes and tomato sauce. Bring to a boil; reduce heat. Stir in the squash; simmer, covered, until squash is tender, 20-25 minutes. Stir in the vinegar.
3. If desired, top individual servings with chopped avocado, Greek yogurt and shredded mozzarella cheese.
1 cup: 261 cal., 8g fat (3g sat. fat), 35mg chol., 704mg sod., 32g carb. (6g sugars, 8g fiber), 18g pro. **Diabetic exchanges:** 2 starch, 2 lean meat.

TEST KITCHEN TIPS

If you're short on time, check the local produce market, as many now offer peeled and cubed butternut squash.

Unexpected company? Ladle the chili over spiral pasta or macaroni to stretch the servings.

Vinegar, added just before serving, helps brighten many dishes, especially rich or fatty ones.

BRATWURST SOUP

I came up with this hearty recipe one day when I had some leftover bratwurst. It's been a favorite of my husband's ever since, and it is requested whenever the guys are hanging out at our house.
—Anna Miller, Churdan, IA

- -

Prep: 10 min. • **Cook:** 25 min.
Makes: 8 servings (2 qt.)

- 1 lb. uncooked bratwurst links, casings removed
- ½ cup chopped onion
- 1 medium carrot, chopped
- 2 cans (15½ oz. each) navy beans, rinsed and drained
- ¼ cup pickled jalapeno slices, chopped
- ½ tsp. pepper
- 2 cups reduced-sodium chicken broth
- ¼ cup all-purpose flour
- 1½ cups 2% milk, divided
- 12 slices American cheese

1. In a Dutch oven, cook and crumble bratwurst with onion and carrot over medium heat until meat is no longer pink, 5-7 minutes; drain.
2. Stir in beans, jalapeno, pepper and broth; bring to a boil. Whisk together the flour and ½ cup milk until smooth; stir into soup. Bring to a boil, stirring constantly; cook and stir until thickened, about 5 minutes. Gradually stir in the remaining milk. Add cheese; cook and stir over low heat until melted.
1 cup: 468 cal., 25g fat (11g sat. fat), 53mg chol., 1322mg sod., 33g carb. (5g sugars, 6g fiber), 25g pro.

GRANDMA'S FAVORITE

SIDE DISHES

When struggling to round out a menu, look no further than Grandma's apron strings. Indulge in these longtime staples that turn any meal into a special occasion.

GRANDMA'S
CORNBREAD
DRESSING

GRANDMA'S CORNBREAD DRESSING

Growing up, we didn't have turkey. We had chicken chopped and baked in my grandmother's dressing. Now we leave out the chicken and keep the must-have cornbread dressing.
—Suzanne Mohme, Bastrop, TX

Prep: 40 min. + cooling • **Bake:** 45 min.
Makes: 12 servings

- 1 cup all-purpose flour
- 1 cup cornmeal
- 2 tsp. baking powder
- 1 tsp. salt
- 2 large eggs, room temperature
- 1 cup buttermilk
- ¼ cup canola oil

DRESSING
- 1 Tbsp. canola oil
- 1 medium onion, chopped
- 2 celery ribs, chopped
- 3 large eggs
- 2 cans (10¾ oz. each) condensed cream of chicken soup, undiluted
- 3 tsp. poultry seasoning
- 1 tsp. pepper
- ½ tsp. salt
- 2 cups chicken broth

1. Preheat oven to 400°. In a large bowl, whisk flour, cornmeal, baking powder and salt. In another bowl, whisk the eggs and buttermilk. Pour oil into an 8-in. ovenproof skillet; place skillet in oven 4 minutes.
2. Meanwhile, add the buttermilk mixture to flour mixture; stir just until moistened.
3. Carefully tilt and rotate the skillet to coat bottom with oil; add the batter. Bake until a toothpick inserted in the center comes out clean, 20-25 minutes. Cool completely in pan on a wire rack.
4. Reduce oven setting to 350°. For dressing, in a large skillet, heat oil over medium-high heat. Add the onion and celery; cook and stir until tender, 4-6 minutes. Remove from heat. Coarsely crumble cornbread into skillet; toss to combine. In a small bowl, whisk the eggs, condensed soup and seasonings; stir into the bread mixture. Stir in broth.
5. Transfer to a greased 13x9-in. baking dish. Bake 45-55 minutes or until lightly browned.
⅔ cup: 236 cal., 12g fat (2g sat. fat), 83mg chol., 969mg sod., 25g carb. (2g sugars, 2g fiber), 7g pro.

MOLDED CRANBERRY-ORANGE SALAD

MOLDED CRANBERRY-ORANGE SALAD

I take this dish to many potlucks, and people always "ooh" and "aah" at how beautiful it is. Feel free to top with a little whipped cream for added appeal.
—Carol Mead, Los Alamos, NM

Prep: 20 min. + chilling • **Makes:** 12 servings

- 1 tsp. unflavored gelatin
- 1 Tbsp. plus 1 cup cold water, divided
- 1 cup boiling water
- 1 pkg. (3 oz.) raspberry gelatin
- 3 cups (12 oz.) fresh or thawed frozen cranberries, divided
- 2 medium apples, cut into wedges
- 1 medium navel orange, peeled
- 1 cup sugar
- ½ cup chopped walnuts
- ½ cup finely chopped celery

1. Sprinkle unflavored gelatin over 1 Tbsp. cold water; let stand 1 minute. Add boiling water and raspberry gelatin; stir until gelatin is dissolved, about 2 minutes. Stir in the remaining cold water. Refrigerate until thickened, about 45 minutes.
2. Pulse 2⅓ cups cranberries, apples and orange in a food processor until chopped. Transfer to a small bowl; stir in sugar. Stir fruit mixture into thickened gelatin. Fold in the walnuts, celery and the remaining whole cranberries.
3. Coat a 10-in. fluted tube pan, an 8-cup ring mold or two 4-cup molds with cooking spray; pour in gelatin mixture. Cover and refrigerate overnight or until firm. Unmold onto a platter.
½ cup: 154 cal., 3g fat (0 sat. fat), 0 chol., 21mg sod., 32g carb. (28g sugars, 2g fiber), 2g pro.

PERFECT WINTER SALAD

This is my most-requested salad recipe. It is delicious as a main dish with grilled chicken breast or as a side salad. I think it's so good, I sometimes eat it at the end of the meal instead of dessert!

—DeNae Shewmake, Burnsville, MN

Takes: 20 min.
Makes: 12 servings

- ¼ cup reduced-fat mayonnaise
- ¼ cup maple syrup
- 3 Tbsp. white wine vinegar
- 2 Tbsp. minced shallot
- 2 tsp. sugar
- ½ cup canola oil
- 2 pkg. (5 oz. each) spring mix salad greens
- 2 medium tart apples, thinly sliced
- 1 cup dried cherries
- 1 cup pecan halves
- ¼ cup thinly sliced red onion

1. In a small bowl, mix first 5 ingredients; gradually whisk in canola oil until blended. Refrigerate, covered, until serving.
2. To serve, place remaining ingredients in a large bowl; toss with dressing.

1 cup: 235 cal., 18g fat (1g sat. fat), 2mg chol., 47mg sod., 20g carb. (15g sugars, 2g fiber), 2g pro.

MALLOW-TOPPED SWEET POTATOES

MALLOW-TOPPED SWEET POTATOES

My grandmother served this sweet potato casserole during special occasions. The puffy marshmallow topping gives the dish a festive look, and spices enhance the sweet potato flavor.

—Edna Hoffman, Hebron, IN

Prep: 40 min. • **Bake:** 45 min.
Makes: 12 servings

- 4 lbs. sweet potatoes (about 5 large), peeled and cut into 1-in. pieces
- 1 cup 2% milk
- 6 Tbsp. butter, softened
- ½ cup packed brown sugar
- 1 large egg
- 1½ tsp. ground cinnamon
- 1½ tsp. vanilla extract
- ¾ tsp. ground allspice
- ½ tsp. salt
- ¼ tsp. ground nutmeg
- 10 large marshmallows, halved lengthwise

1. Preheat oven to 350°. Place the sweet potatoes in a 6-qt. stockpot; add water to cover. Bring to a boil. Reduce heat; cook, uncovered, until tender, 15-20 minutes. Drain potatoes; place in a large bowl.
2. Beat potatoes until smooth. Add the next 9 ingredients; beat until blended.
3. Spread into a greased shallow 2½-qt. baking dish. Bake, uncovered, until heated through, 40-45 minutes. Increase oven setting to 425°.
4. Top casserole with marshmallows. Bake until the marshmallows are lightly browned, 3-4 minutes.

⅔ cup: 312 cal., 7g fat (4g sat. fat), 36mg chol., 201mg sod., 59g carb. (35g sugars, 3g fiber), 4g pro.

TEST KITCHEN TIP

Light brown sugar has a delicate flavor while the dark variety has a stronger molasses flavor. Feel free to use them interchangeably in recipes.

POTLUCK GERMAN POTATO SALAD

This is a big hit at church potlucks. One man says he only comes so he can eat the potato salad I bring!
—Kathleen Rabe, Kiel, WI

Prep: 20 min. • **Cook:** 25 min.
Makes: 12 servings

- 3 lbs. small Yukon Gold potatoes, unpeeled (about 10)
- 2 celery ribs, chopped
- 1 small onion, chopped
- 1 cup water
- ½ cup white vinegar
- ¾ cup sugar
- 1 Tbsp. cornstarch
- ¼ tsp. salt
- ¼ tsp. pepper
- ½ lb. bacon strips, cooked and crumbled

1. Place potatoes in a large saucepan; add water to cover. Bring to a boil. Reduce heat; simmer, uncovered, 12-15 minutes or just until tender. Add celery and onion; continue cooking until vegetables are tender, about 5 minutes longer. Drain; set aside.
2. Meanwhile, in a small saucepan, whisk together next 6 ingredients. Bring to a boil; cook until thickened, about 2 minutes.
3. When cool enough to handle, slice the potatoes; return to large saucepan with the celery and onions. Add the vinegar mixture, tossing to combine. Add the bacon. Simmer mixture until heated through, 10-12 minutes. Serve warm.

⅔ cup: 194 cal., 3g fat (1g sat. fat), 7mg chol., 181mg sod., 39g carb. (15g sugars, 2g fiber), 5g pro.

EMILY'S HONEY LIME COLESLAW

Here's a refreshing take on slaw with a honey-lime vinaigrette rather than the traditional mayo. It's a great take-along for all those summer picnics.
—Emily Tyra, Traverse City, MI

Prep: 20 min. + chilling • **Makes:** 8 servings

- 1½ tsp. grated lime zest
- ¼ cup lime juice
- 2 Tbsp. honey
- 1 garlic clove, minced
- ½ tsp. salt
- ¼ tsp. pepper
- ¼ tsp. crushed red pepper flakes
- 3 Tbsp. canola oil
- 1 small head red cabbage (about ¾ lb.), shredded
- 1 cup shredded carrots (about 2 medium carrots)
- 2 green onions, thinly sliced
- ½ cup fresh cilantro leaves

Whisk together the first 7 ingredients until smooth. Gradually whisk in oil until blended. Combine the cabbage, carrots and green onions; toss with lime mixture to lightly coat. Refrigerate, covered, 2 hours. Sprinkle with fresh cilantro.

½ cup: 86 cal., 5g fat (0 sat. fat), 0 chol., 170mg sod., 10g carb. (7g sugars, 2g fiber), 1g pro. **Diabetic exchanges:** 1 vegetable, 1 fat.

POTLUCK GERMAN POTATO SALAD

SUMMER'S BEST BAKED BEANS

SUMMER'S BEST BAKED BEANS

We choose this family recipe for summer holidays, picnics and parties because it's a hearty twist on an old favorite. It has a nice sweetness that goes well with grilled foods.
—Wendy Hodorowski, Bellaire, OH

Prep: 10 min. • **Bake:** 55 min.
Makes: 8 servings

- ½ lb. ground beef
- 1 large onion, finely chopped
- ½ cup sugar
- ½ cup packed brown sugar
- ½ cup ketchup
- ½ cup barbecue sauce
- 2 Tbsp. yellow mustard
- 2 Tbsp. molasses
- ½ tsp. chili powder
- 2 cans (13.7 oz. each) beans with tomato sauce
- ½ lb. bacon strips, cooked and crumbled

1. Preheat oven to 350°. In a large skillet, cook beef and onion over medium heat 6-8 minutes or until beef is no longer pink, breaking up beef into crumbles; drain. Stir in sugars, ketchup, barbecue sauce, mustard, molasses and chili powder. Add beans and crumbled bacon.

2. Transfer to a greased 13x9-in. baking dish. Bake, covered, 45 minutes. Bake, uncovered, 10-15 minutes longer or until baked beans are heated through.
¾ cup: 323 cal., 8g fat (3g sat. fat), 28mg chol., 970mg sod., 51g carb. (41g sugars, 4g fiber), 14g pro.

SAUERKRAUT LATKES

Sauerkraut in potato pancakes might seem like an unusual combination, but it's one worth trying. The apples mellow the tang for an wonderfully pleasant flavor.
—Aysha Schurman, Ammon, ID

Prep: 20 min. • **Cook:** 5 min./batch
Makes: 2½ dozen

- 3 lbs. russet potatoes, peeled and shredded
- 1½ cups shredded peeled apples
- 1½ cups sauerkraut, rinsed and well drained
- 6 large eggs, lightly beaten
- 6 Tbsp. all-purpose flour
- 2 tsp. salt
- 1½ tsp. pepper
- ¾ cup canola oil
  Optional: Sour cream and chopped green onions

1. In a large bowl, combine the shredded potatoes, apples, sauerkraut and eggs. Combine the flour, salt and pepper; stir into the potato mixture.

2. Heat 2 Tbsp. oil in a large nonstick skillet over medium heat. Drop the batter by ¼ cupfuls into oil; press lightly to flatten. Fry in batches until golden brown on both sides, using remaining oil as needed. Drain on paper towels. Top with sour cream and green onions if desired.
3 latkes: 306 cal., 20g fat (2g sat. fat), 127mg chol., 658mg sod., 27g carb. (5g sugars, 3g fiber), 6g pro.

RED, WHITE & BLUE SALAD

Our striking flag salad drew plenty of attention at our Independence Day party. I use gelatin to help create the shimmering stripes. It looks complicated but it's so easy.
—Laurie Neverman, Denmark, WI

Prep: 30 min. + chilling • **Makes:** 16 servings

- 1 pkg. (3 oz.) berry blue gelatin
- 2 cups boiling water, divided
- 2½ cups cold water, divided
- 1 cup fresh blueberries
- 1 envelope unflavored gelatin
- 1 cup heavy whipping cream
- 6 Tbsp. sugar
- 2 cups sour cream
- 1 tsp. vanilla extract
- 1 pkg. (3 oz.) raspberry gelatin
- 1 cup fresh raspberries
  Optional: Whipped topping and additional berries

1. Dissolve berry blue gelatin in 1 cup boiling water; stir in 1 cup cold water. Add the blueberries. Pour into a 3-qt. serving bowl. Refrigerate until firm, about 1 hour.
2. In a saucepan, sprinkle the unflavored gelatin over ½ cup cold water; let stand for 1 minute. Add cream and sugar; cook and stir over low heat until dissolved. Cool to room temperature. Whisk in sour cream and vanilla. Spoon over blue layer. Refrigerate until firm.
3. Dissolve raspberry gelatin in remaining hot water; stir in remaining cold water. Add raspberries. Spoon over cream layer. Chill until set. Top with whipped topping and berries if desired.
1 serving: 179 cal., 11g fat (7g sat. fat), 40mg chol., 46mg sod., 18g carb. (16g sugars, 1g fiber), 3g pro.

RED, WHITE
& BLUE SALAD

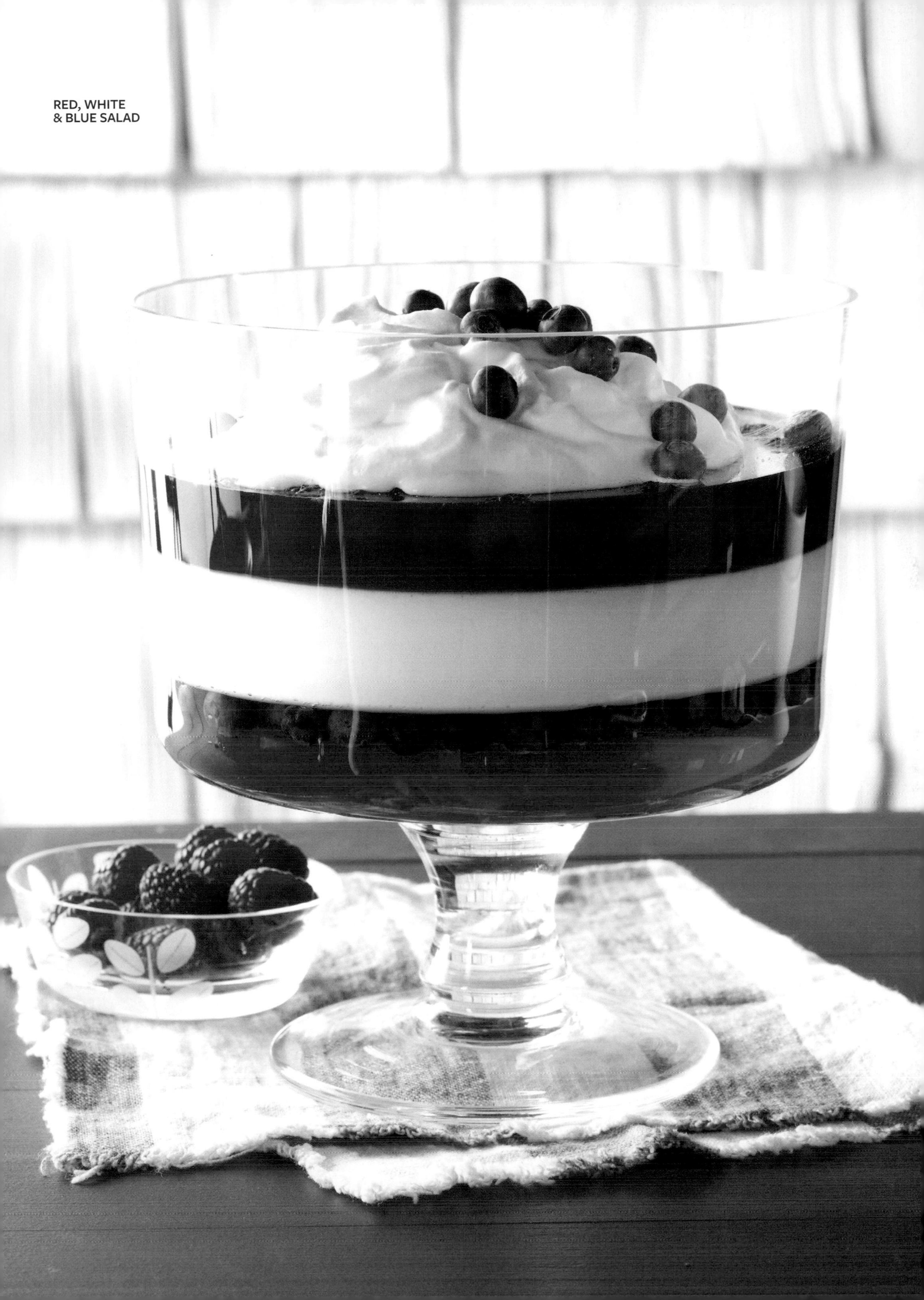

SICILIAN POTATO SALAD

Fresh basil is the star of this mayo-free, Italian-inspired take on potato salad.
—Sue Falk, Sterling Heights, MI

- -

Prep: 20 min. • **Cook:** 20 min.
Makes: 26 servings

- 10 small russet potatoes, unpeeled
- 1½ tsp. salt, divided
- ½ lb. fresh green beans, cut into 1½-in. pieces
- ¼ tsp. pepper
- 2 medium cucumbers, halved lengthwise and cut into ¼-in. slices
- ½ lb. cherry tomatoes, halved
- 1 large red onion, halved and thinly sliced
- 1 cup thinly sliced fresh basil leaves, divided
- ½ cup olive oil
- 4 Tbsp. cider vinegar
- 3 garlic cloves, minced

1. Place potatoes and ½ tsp. salt in a Dutch oven; add water to cover. Bring to a boil. Reduce heat; cook, uncovered, until tender, 12-15 minutes. Drain; rinse with cold water. Pat dry.

2. Meanwhile, in a small saucepan, bring 1 cup water to a boil. Add beans; cook, uncovered, for 3-4 minutes or just until crisp-tender. Drain; immediately drop into ice water. Drain and pat dry.

3. Peel and cube the potatoes; sprinkle with the remaining salt and the pepper. Transfer to a serving bowl. Add beans, cucumbers, tomatoes, onion and ¾ cup basil leaves. Whisk together oil, vinegar and garlic. Drizzle over vegetables; toss to coat. Sprinkle with remaining basil.

¾ cup: 96 cal., 4g fat (1g sat. fat), 0 chol., 143mg sod., 13g carb. (2g sugars, 2g fiber), 2g pro. **Diabetic exchanges:** 1 starch, 1 fat.

GREEN BEAN CASSEROLE

This classic side dish casserole has always been one of my favorite dishes—it's so simple to put together! You can make it before any guests arrive and keep it refrigerated until baking time.
—Anna Baker, Blaine, WA

- -

Prep: 15 min. • **Bake:** 35 min.
Makes: 10 servings

- 2 cans (10¾ oz. each) condensed cream of mushroom soup, undiluted
- 1 cup whole milk
- 2 tsp. soy sauce
- ⅛ tsp. pepper
- 2 pkg. (16 oz. each) frozen green beans, cooked and drained
- 1 can (6 oz.) french-fried onions, divided

1. In a bowl, combine soup, milk, soy sauce and pepper. Gently stir in beans. Spoon half of the mixture into a 13x9-in. baking dish. Sprinkle with half of the onions. Spoon the remaining bean mixture over the top. Sprinkle with remaining onions.

2. Bake at 350° until heated through and onions are brown and crispy, 30-35 minutes.

1 cup: 163 cal., 11g fat (3g sat. fat), 5mg chol., 485mg sod., 14g carb. (2g sugars, 1g fiber), 2g pro.

SICILIAN POTATO SALAD

MASHED POTATOES WITH GARLIC-OLIVE OIL

LAYERED SALAD FOR A CROWD

This salad is a favorite with my three sons. I took it to a luncheon honoring our school district's food service manager, and she asked for the recipe! I like to make the dressing the day before so the flavors blend nicely together.
—Linda Ashley, Leesburg, GA

Takes: 20 min. • **Makes:** 20 servings

- 1 cup mayonnaise
- ¼ cup whole milk
- 2 tsp. dill weed
- ½ tsp. seasoning blend
- 1 bunch romaine, torn
- 2 medium carrots, grated
- 1 cup chopped red onion
- 1 medium cucumber, sliced
- 1 pkg. (10 oz.) frozen peas, thawed
- 1½ cups shredded cheddar cheese
- 8 bacon strips, cooked and crumbled

1. For dressing, in a small bowl, whisk the mayonnaise, milk, dill and seasoning blend. In a 4-qt. clear glass serving bowl, layer the romaine, carrots, onion and cucumber (do not toss). Pour dressing over the top; sprinkle with peas, cheese and bacon. Cover and refrigerate until serving.

Note: This recipe was tested with Nature's Seasons seasoning blend by Morton. Look for it in the spice aisle.

⅔ cup: 151 cal., 13g fat (4g sat. fat), 16mg chol., 216mg sod., 5g carb. (2g sugars, 1g fiber), 4g pro.

MASHED POTATOES WITH GARLIC-OLIVE OIL

Garlic mashed potatoes are high on our love list. To intensify the flavor, I combine garlic and olive oil in the food processor and drizzle it on top of the potatoes.
—Emory Doty, Jasper, GA

Takes: 30 min. • **Makes:** 12 servings

- 4 lbs. red potatoes, quartered
- ½ cup olive oil
- 2 garlic cloves
- ⅔ cup heavy whipping cream
- ¼ cup butter, softened
- 2 tsp. salt
- ½ tsp. pepper
- ⅔ to ¾ cup whole milk
- 3 green onions, chopped
- ¾ cup grated Parmesan cheese, optional

1. Place potatoes in a Dutch oven; add water to cover. Bring to a boil. Reduce heat; cook, uncovered, until tender, 15-20 minutes. Meanwhile, place oil and garlic in a small food processor; process until blended.

2. Drain potatoes; return to pan. Mash potatoes, gradually adding cream, butter, salt, pepper and enough milk to reach desired consistency. Stir in green onions. Serve with garlic olive oil and, if desired, Parmesan cheese.

Note: For food safety purposes, prepare garlic olive oil just before serving; do not store leftover oil mixture.

¾ cup mashed potatoes with 1 Tbsp. cheese and about 2 tsp. oil mixture: 299 cal., 20g fat (8g sat. fat), 31mg chol., 533mg sod., 26g carb. (3g sugars, 3g fiber), 5g pro.

GRANDMA'S FAVORITE

MAIN COURSES

Pull up a chair and get ready for a mouthwatering meal that stars one of Grandma's longtime favorites. Featuring the savory goodness you've come to expect, these entrees combine the convenience today's cooks need with the flavors they love.

HONEY
WALLEYE

1. Bring 4 cups water to a boil in a large saucepan. Add asparagus; cook, uncovered, for 3 minutes or until crisp-tender. Drain and immediately place the asparagus in ice water. Drain and pat dry. Set aside.
2. Spread the turkey cutlets with Dijon-mayonnaise. Layer with ham, cheese and asparagus. Sprinkle with poultry seasoning and pepper. Roll up tightly and wrap with the bacon.
3. Cook the roulades in a large skillet over medium-high heat until bacon is crisp and turkey is no longer pink, turning occasionally, 12-15 minutes. Combine sauce ingredients; serve with roulades.
1 roulade with 1 Tbsp. sauce: 224 cal., 11g fat (5g sat. fat), 64mg chol., 1075mg sod., 2g carb. (1g sugars, 0 fiber), 25g pro.

GRANDMA'S SWEDISH MEATBALLS
My mother made these hearty meatballs when we were growing up, and now my kids love them, too. My daughter likes to help shake the meatballs in flour.
—Karin Ness, Big Lake, MN

- -

Takes: 30 min. • **Makes:** 4 servings

    1   large egg, lightly beaten
    ½   cup crushed saltines
        (about 10 crackers)
    ¼   tsp. seasoned salt
    ¼   tsp. pepper
    ½   lb. ground beef
    ½   lb. bulk pork sausage
    ¼   cup plus 2 Tbsp. all-
        purpose flour, divided
   2½   cups reduced-sodium
        beef broth, divided
        Hot mashed potatoes
        Minced fresh parsley, optional

1. Mix first 4 ingredients. Add the beef and sausage; mix lightly but thoroughly. Gently shape into 1-in. balls; toss with ¼ cup flour, coating lightly.
2. In a large skillet, brown meatballs over medium-high heat. Add 2 cups broth; bring to a boil. Reduce heat; simmer, covered, until meatballs are cooked through, 5-6 minutes.
3. Remove meatballs with a slotted spoon. Mix the remaining flour and broth until smooth; add to pan. Bring to a boil; cook and stir until thickened, 1-2 minutes. Return meatballs to pan; heat through. Serve with mashed potatoes. If desired, sprinkle with minced parsley.
1 serving: 348 cal., 21g fat (7g sat. fat), 115mg chol., 846mg sod., 17g carb. (1g sugars, 1g fiber), 21g pro.

HONEY WALLEYE
Our state is known as the Land of 10,000 Lakes, so fishing is a favorite recreational activity here. This recipe is a quick way to prepare all the fresh walleye hooked by the anglers in our family.
—Kitty McCue, St. Louis Park, MN

- -

Takes: 20 min. • **Makes:** 6 servings

    1   large egg
    2   tsp. honey
    2   cups crushed Ritz crackers
         (about 45 to 50)
    ½   tsp. salt
   1½   lbs. walleye fillets
    ⅓   to ½ cup canola oil
         Lemon wedge and minced fresh
         parsley, optional

1. In a shallow bowl, beat egg; add honey. In a shallow dish, combine crackers and salt. Dip fish in egg mixture, then in cracker mixture; turn until coated.
2. In a cast-iron or other heavy skillet, cook fillets in oil over medium heat until golden and fish flakes easily with a fork, 3-5 minutes on each side. If desired, top with parsley and serve with lemon wedges.

3 oz. cooked fish: 389 cal., 22g fat (3g sat. fat), 133mg chol., 514mg sod., 23g carb. (5g sugars, 1g fiber), 25g pro.

TURKEY CLUB ROULADES
Need an elegant meal on short notice? Try these short-prep roulades. If you only have chicken breast on hand, lightly pound them flat and use them instead of the turkey.
—*Taste of Home* Test Kitchen

- -

Prep: 20 min. • **Cook:** 15 min.
Makes: 8 servings

    ¾   lb. fresh asparagus, trimmed
    8   turkey breast cutlets (about 1 lb.)
    1   Tbsp. Dijon-mayonnaise blend
    8   slices deli ham
    8   slices provolone cheese
    ½   tsp. poultry seasoning
    ½   tsp. pepper
    8   bacon strips
SAUCE
    ⅔   cup Dijon-mayonnaise blend
    4   tsp. 2% milk
    ¼   tsp. poultry seasoning

GRANDMA'S
SWEDISH
MEATBALLS

GRAM'S FRIED CHICKEN

As a boy, I wolfed down my grandmother's fried chicken. I never knew how she made it, but my recipe using crispy potato flakes is pretty close.
—David Nelson, Lincolnton, NC

- -

Prep: 20 min. + chilling • **Cook:** 10 min.
Makes: 4 servings

- 1 large egg
- 1 cup 2% milk
- 2 cups mashed potato flakes
- 1 Tbsp. garlic powder
- 1 Tbsp. each dried oregano, parsley flakes and minced onion
- ½ tsp. salt
- ¼ tsp. coarsely ground pepper
- 4 boneless skinless chicken breast halves (6 oz. each)
  Oil for frying

1. In a shallow bowl, whisk egg and milk. In another shallow bowl, toss potato flakes with seasonings. Remove half of the mixture and reserve (for a second coat of breading).
2. Pound chicken with a meat mallet to ½-in. thickness. Dip chicken in egg mixture, then in potato mixture, patting to help coating adhere. Arrange chicken in an even layer on a large plate. Cover and refrigerate chicken and remaining egg mixture 1 hour. Discard remaining used potato mixture.
3. In a 12-in. cast-iron or other deep skillet, heat ½ in. of oil over medium heat to 350°. For the second coat of breading, dip chicken in remaining egg mixture, then in unused potato mixture; pat to coat. Fry the chicken for 4-5 minutes on each side or until golden brown and chicken is no longer pink. Drain on paper towels.

1 chicken breast half: 469 cal., 28g fat (3g sat. fat), 121mg chol., 269mg sod., 16g carb. (3g sugars, 2g fiber), 38g pro.

MEAT SAUCE FOR
SPAGHETTI

MEAT SAUCE FOR SPAGHETTI

Here's a hearty meat sauce that easily turns ordinary spaghetti and garlic bread into a memorable feast. If you do not have any spaghetti noodles on hand, no problem! I have successfully swirled up this sauce with nearly every pasta shape in my pantry.
—Mary Tallman, Arbor Vitae, WI

- -

Prep: 30 min. • **Cook:** 8 hours
Makes: 9 servings

- 1 lb. ground beef
- 1 lb. bulk Italian sausage
- 1 can (28 oz.) crushed tomatoes, undrained
- 1 medium green pepper, chopped
- 1 medium onion, chopped
- 2 medium carrots, finely chopped
- 1 cup water
- 1 can (8 oz.) tomato sauce
- 1 can (6 oz.) tomato paste
- 1 Tbsp. brown sugar
- 1 Tbsp. Italian seasoning
- 2 garlic cloves, minced
- ½ tsp. salt
- ¼ tsp. pepper
  Hot cooked spaghetti

1. In a large skillet, cook beef and sausage over medium heat until no longer pink; drain.
2. Transfer to a 5-qt. slow cooker. Stir in the tomatoes, green pepper, onion, carrots, water, tomato sauce, tomato paste, brown sugar, Italian seasoning, garlic, salt and pepper. Cover and cook on low until bubbly, 8-10 hours. Serve with spaghetti.

Freeze option: Do not cook spaghetti. Freeze meat sauce in freezer containers. To use, partially thaw in refrigerator overnight. Cook spaghetti according to the package directions. Place sauce in a large skillet; heat through, stirring occasionally and adding a little water if necessary. Serve over spaghetti.

1 cup: 286 cal., 17g fat (6g sat. fat), 58mg chol., 767mg sod., 17g carb. (9g sugars, 4g fiber), 18g pro.

"When in a hurry I leave out the beef and sausage and add frozen meatballs. It still gets rave reviews."
—DPINKHAM4, TASTEOFHOME.COM

COMPANY TURKEY POTPIE

Here's our smart spin on potpie, filled with turkey, autumn vegetables and a creamy herb sauce. Best of all, there's no crust to make—just top with prepared phyllo dough.
—*Taste of Home* Test Kitchen

- -

Prep: 1 hour • **Bake:** 10 min.
Makes: 6 servings

- ½ **lb. sliced baby portobello mushrooms**
- 2 **shallots, chopped**
- 2 **tsp. olive oil**
- 2 **cups cubed peeled butternut squash**
- 1 **cup chopped sweet red pepper**
- ½ **cup sliced fennel bulb**
- 2 **cups reduced-sodium chicken broth, divided**
- ⅓ **cup all-purpose flour**
- ½ **cup 2% milk**
- 3 **cups cubed cooked turkey breast**
- 2 **Tbsp. sherry or additional reduced-sodium chicken broth**
- 1 **tsp. rubbed sage**
- ½ **tsp. salt**
- ½ **tsp. dried thyme**
- ¼ **tsp. pepper**
- 10 **sheets phyllo dough (14x9-in. size) Refrigerated butter-flavored spray**

1. In a large skillet, saute mushrooms and shallots in oil until tender. Add the squash, red pepper and fennel; saute 5 minutes longer. Add ¼ cup broth. Cover and cook over medium-low heat until vegetables are tender, about 15 minutes.
2. Sprinkle flour over vegetables; cook and stir for 1 minute. Gradually add the milk and remaining broth. Bring to a boil; cook and stir until thickened, 1-2 minutes. Stir in the turkey, sherry and seasonings; heat through. Transfer to a 2-qt. baking dish coated with cooking spray.
3. Stack all 10 phyllo sheets. Roll up, starting with a long side; cut into ½-in. strips. Place strips in a large bowl and toss to separate; spritz with butter-flavored spray. Arrange over the turkey mixture; spritz again. Bake, uncovered, at 425° until golden brown, 10-15 minutes.
1 cup: 275 cal., 4g fat (1g sat. fat), 62mg chol., 544mg sod., 33g carb. (6g sugars, 5g fiber), 28g pro. **Diabetic exchanges:** 3 lean meat, 2 starch.

COMPANY TURKEY POTPIE

GERMAN BRAT SEAFOOD BOIL

This meal-in-one features grilled bratwurst, which adds a smoky flavor to corn, potatoes and fish for a hearty meal that's always a hit.
—Trisha Kruse, Eagle, ID

- -

Prep: 25 min. • **Cook:** 30 min.
Makes: 6 servings

- 1 **pkg. (19 oz.) uncooked bratwurst links**
- 1 **medium onion, quartered**
- 2 **qt. water**
- 2 **bottles (12 oz. each) beer or 3 cups reduced-sodium chicken broth**
- ½ **cup seafood seasoning**
- 5 **medium ears sweet corn, cut into 2-in. pieces**
- 2 **lbs. small red potatoes**
- 1 **medium lemon, halved**
- 1 **lb. cod fillet, cut into 1-in. pieces Coarsely ground pepper**

1. Grill bratwurst, covered, over medium heat, turning frequently, until meat is no longer pink, 15-20 minutes. Grill the onion, covered, until lightly browned, 3-4 minutes on each side. Cut bratwurst into 2-in. pieces.
2. In a stockpot, combine water, beer and seafood seasoning; add the corn, potatoes, lemon, bratwurst and onion. Bring to a boil. Reduce heat; simmer, uncovered, until the potatoes are tender, 15-20 minutes. Stir in cod; cook until the fish flakes easily with a fork, 4-6 minutes. Drain; transfer to a large serving bowl. Sprinkle with pepper.
1 serving: 553 cal., 28g fat (9g sat. fat), 95mg chol., 1620mg sod., 46g carb. (8g sugars, 5g fiber), 30g pro.

ROAST PORK WITH
APPLES & ONIONS

ROAST PORK WITH APPLES & ONIONS

Here, the sweetness of apples and onions really complements roast pork. With its crisp skin and melt-in-your-mouth flavor, this is my family's favorite weekend dinner.
—Lily Julow, Lawrenceville, GA

- -

Prep: 30 min. • **Bake:** 45 min. + standing
Makes: 8 servings

- 1 boneless pork loin roast (2 lbs.)
- ¼ tsp. salt
- ¼ tsp. pepper
- 1 Tbsp. olive oil
- 3 large Golden Delicious apples, cut into 1-in. wedges
- 2 large onions, cut into ¾-in. wedges
- 5 garlic cloves, peeled
- 1 Tbsp. minced fresh rosemary or 1 tsp. dried rosemary, crushed

1. Preheat oven to 350°. Sprinkle roast with salt and pepper. In a large nonstick skillet, heat oil over medium heat; brown roast on all sides. Transfer to a roasting pan coated with cooking spray. Place apples, onions and garlic around roast; sprinkle with rosemary.
2. Roast until a thermometer inserted in pork reads 145°, 45-55 minutes, turning the apples, onion and garlic once. Remove from oven; tent with foil. Let stand 10 minutes before slicing roast. Serve roast pork with the apple mixture.
1 serving: 210 cal., 7g fat (2g sat. fat), 57mg chol., 109mg sod., 14g carb. (9g sugars, 2g fiber), 23g pro. **Diabetic exchanges:** 3 lean meat, 1 starch, ½ fat.

WHITE SEAFOOD LASAGNA

We enjoy lasagna with shrimp and scallops as part of the traditional Italian Feast of the Seven Fishes. Every bite delivers a tasty jewel from the sea.
—Joe Colamonico, North Charleston, SC

- -

Prep: 1 hour • **Bake:** 40 min. + standing
Makes: 12 servings

- 9 uncooked lasagna noodles
- 1 Tbsp. butter
- 1 lb. uncooked shrimp (31 to 40 per lb.), peeled and deveined
- 1 lb. bay scallops
- 5 garlic cloves, minced
- ¼ cup white wine
- 1 Tbsp. lemon juice
- 1 lb. fresh crabmeat

CHEESE SAUCE
- ¼ cup butter, cubed
- ¼ cup all-purpose flour
- 3 cups 2% milk

WHITE SEAFOOD LASAGNA

- 1 cup shredded part-skim mozzarella cheese
- ½ cup grated Parmesan cheese
- ½ tsp. salt
- ¼ tsp. pepper
  Dash ground nutmeg

RICOTTA MIXTURE
- 1 carton (15 oz.) part-skim ricotta cheese
- 1 pkg. (10 oz.) frozen chopped spinach, thawed and squeezed dry
- 1 cup shredded part-skim mozzarella cheese
- ½ cup grated Parmesan cheese
- ½ cup seasoned bread crumbs
- 1 large egg, lightly beaten

TOPPING
- 1 cup shredded part-skim mozzarella cheese
- ¼ cup grated Parmesan cheese
  Minced fresh parsley

1. Preheat oven to 350°. Cook lasagna noodles according to package directions; drain.
2. Meanwhile, in a large skillet, heat butter over medium heat. Add shrimp and scallops in batches; cook 2-4 minutes or until shrimp turn pink and scallops are firm and opaque. Remove from pan.

3. Add garlic to same pan; cook 1 minute. Add wine and lemon juice, stirring to loosen browned bits from pan. Bring to a boil; cook 1-2 minutes or until liquid is reduced by half. Add crab; heat through. Stir in the shrimp and scallops.
4. For the cheese sauce, melt butter over medium heat in a large saucepan. Stir in flour until smooth; gradually whisk in milk. Bring to a boil, stirring constantly; cook and stir for 1-2 minutes or until thickened. Remove from the heat; stir in the remaining cheese sauce ingredients. In a large bowl, combine ricotta cheese mixture ingredients; stir in 1 cup cheese sauce.
5. Spread ½ cup cheese sauce into a greased 13x9-in. baking dish. Layer with 3 noodles, half of the ricotta mixture, half the seafood mixture and ⅔ cup cheese sauce. Repeat layers. Top with remaining noodles and cheese sauce. Sprinkle with remaining mozzarella cheese and Parmesan cheese.
6. Bake, uncovered, 40-50 minutes or until bubbly and top is golden brown. Let stand 10 minutes before serving. Sprinkle with fresh parsley.
1 piece: 448 cal., 19g fat (11g sat. fat), 158mg chol., 957mg sod., 29g carb. (5g sugars, 2g fiber), 39g pro.

FLOUNDER WITH SHRIMP STUFFING

The delicious shrimp-herb stuffing makes this fish recipe company-special. But it really isn't hard to make. Our family enjoys fish, so we eat this often.
—Marie Forte, Raritan, NJ

- -

Prep: 30 min. • **Bake:** 20 min.
Makes: 6 servings

STUFFING
- 6 Tbsp. butter, cubed
- 1 small onion, finely chopped
- ¼ cup finely chopped celery
- ¼ cup finely chopped green pepper
- 1 lb. uncooked shrimp, peeled, deveined and chopped
- ¼ cup beef broth
- 1 tsp. diced pimientos, drained
- 1 tsp. Worcestershire sauce
- ½ tsp. dill weed
- ½ tsp. minced chives
- ⅛ tsp. salt
- ⅛ tsp. cayenne pepper
- 1½ cups soft bread crumbs

FISH
- 6 flounder fillets (3 oz. each)
- 5 Tbsp. butter, melted
- 2 Tbsp. lemon juice
- 1 tsp. minced fresh parsley
- ½ tsp. paprika
- Salt and pepper to taste

1. Preheat the oven to 375°. In a large skillet, melt butter. Add the onion, celery and green pepper; saute until tender. Add shrimp; cook and stir until shrimp turn pink. Add broth, pimientos, Worcestershire sauce, dill, chives, salt and cayenne; heat through. Remove from heat; stir in bread crumbs.
2. Spoon about ½ cup stuffing onto each fillet; roll up. Place seam side down in a greased 13x9-in. baking dish. Drizzle with the butter and lemon juice. Sprinkle with seasonings. Bake, uncovered, 20-25 minutes or until fish flakes easily with a fork.

1 stuffed fillet: 357 cal., 23g fat (14g sat. fat), 187mg chol., 476mg sod., 9g carb. (1g sugars, 1g fiber), 28g pro.

TURKEY A LA KING

This is a smart way to use up leftover turkey. You might want to make a double batch!
—Mary Gaylord, Balsam Lake, WI

- -

Takes: 25 min. • **Makes:** 6 servings

- 1 medium onion, chopped
- ¾ cup sliced celery
- ¼ cup diced green pepper
- ¼ cup butter, cubed
- ¼ cup all-purpose flour
- 1 tsp. sugar
- 1½ cups chicken broth
- ¼ cup half-and-half cream
- 3 cups cubed cooked turkey or chicken
- 1 can (4 oz.) sliced mushrooms, drained
- 6 slices bread, toasted

1. In a large skillet, saute the onion, celery and green pepper in butter until tender. Stir in flour and sugar until a paste forms.
2. Gradually stir in broth. Bring to a boil; boil until thickened, about 1 minute. Reduce the heat. Add cream, turkey and mushrooms; heat through. Serve with toast.

1 serving: 297 cal., 13g fat (7g sat. fat), 98mg chol., 591mg sod., 21g carb. (4g sugars, 2g fiber), 24g pro.

FLOUNDER WITH SHRIMP STUFFING

SLOW-COOKED RUMP ROAST

CHICKEN DIVAN

This tasty recipe was given to me by a friend years ago, and it's been a family favorite ever since. My daughters enjoy making the dish in their own homes now and get the same enthusiastic compliments I have always received!
—Mary Pat Lucia, North East, PA

- -

Prep: 20 min. • **Bake:** 35 min.
Makes: 10 servings

- ¼ cup plus 1 Tbsp. butter, divided
- ¼ cup all-purpose flour
- 1½ cups half-and-half cream
- ½ cup cooking sherry or water
- 2 cans (10¾ oz. each) condensed cream of chicken soup, undiluted
- 2 pkg. (10 oz. each) frozen cut or chopped broccoli, thawed
- 1 cup cooked rice
- 3 to 4 cups cubed cooked chicken
- 2 cups shredded cheddar cheese
- 1 cup soft bread crumbs

1. In a small saucepan, melt ¼ cup butter. Add flour, stirring until blended. Stir in the cream and cooking sherry or water; cook and stir until thickened and bubbly. Cook and stir 2 more minutes. Blend in soup until smooth; remove from the heat and set aside.
2. Place broccoli in an ungreased 13x9-in. baking dish. Cover with rice and then half of the sauce. Top with chicken. Stir shredded cheese into the remaining sauce; pour over the chicken.
3. Melt the remaining butter and toss with bread crumbs. Sprinkle over the casserole. Bake, uncovered, at 350° for 35-45 minutes or until heated through.

1 cup: 412 cal., 24g fat (12g sat. fat), 98mg chol., 798mg sod., 20g carb. (3g sugars, 3g fiber), 22g pro.

SLOW-COOKED RUMP ROAST

I enjoy a good pot roast, but I was growing tired of the same old thing...so I started experimenting. Simmering this beef roast in horseradish sauce gives it a tangy flavor. Even my littles love the entree with its tender veggies and gravy.
—Mimi Walker, Palmyra, PA

- -

Prep: 10 min. • **Cook:** 8 hours
Makes: 8 servings

- 1 beef rump roast or bottom round roast (3 to 3½ lbs.)
- 2 Tbsp. canola oil
- 4 medium carrots, halved lengthwise and cut into 2-in. pieces
- 3 medium potatoes, peeled and cut into chunks
- 2 small onions, sliced
- ½ cup water
- 6 to 8 Tbsp. horseradish sauce
- ¼ cup red wine vinegar
- ¼ cup Worcestershire sauce
- 2 garlic cloves, minced
- 1½ to 2 tsp. celery salt
- 3 Tbsp. cornstarch
- ⅓ cup cold water

1. Cut roast in half. In a large skillet, brown meat on all sides in oil over medium-high heat; drain. Place carrots and potatoes in a 5-qt. slow cooker. Top with meat and onions. Combine the water, horseradish sauce, vinegar, Worcestershire sauce, garlic and celery salt. Pour over meat. Cover and cook on low until meat and vegetables are tender, about 8 hours.
2. Combine cornstarch and cold water until smooth; stir into slow cooker. Cover and cook on high until gravy is thickened, about 30 minutes.

1 serving: 378 cal., 15g fat (3g sat. fat), 113mg chol., 507mg sod., 23g carb. (6g sugars, 2g fiber), 35g pro. **Diabetic exchanges:** 4 lean meat, 1½ starch, 1 fat.

GRANDMA'S FAVORITE

SUNDAY DINNERS

Gather around the table and settle in for the kind of meal
made famous at Grandma's house. Here, you'll find complete
lineups for casual yet cheery suppers, as well as impressive
menus sure to make memories for years to come.

ROAST CHICKEN WITH CREOLE STUFFING

ROAST CHICKEN WITH CREOLE STUFFING

I've used this recipe ever since I roasted my first chicken. Our whole family looks forward to it. The combination of shrimp, sausage, ham, vegetables and seasonings makes the stuffing unique and delicious.
—Ruth Bates, Temecula, CA

Prep: 50 min. • **Bake:** 3 hours
Makes: 8 servings (8 cups stuffing)

- 1½ cups uncooked brown rice
- 2 Italian sausage links
- 2 Tbsp. vegetable oil
- 1 cup chopped onion
- 5 garlic cloves, minced
- ½ cup diced green pepper
- ½ cup diced sweet red pepper
- 1 can (14½ oz.) diced tomatoes, undrained
- 1 Tbsp. lemon juice
- 1 tsp. dried basil
- ½ tsp. sugar
- ½ tsp. hot pepper sauce
- ½ tsp. chicken bouillon granules
- ¼ tsp. chili powder
- ¼ tsp. pepper
- ⅛ tsp. dried thyme
- 1¼ tsp. salt, divided
- 1 cup diced fully cooked ham
- 1 cup cooked small shrimp, peeled and deveined, optional
- 3 Tbsp. minced fresh parsley
- 1 roasting chicken (5 to 6 lbs.)
- ½ tsp. paprika
  Dash pepper

1. In a large saucepan, cook rice according to package directions. Meanwhile, in a skillet, cook the sausages in oil until a thermometer reads 160°. Remove the sausages, reserving drippings. When cool enough to handle, cut sausages in half lengthwise, then into ¼-in. pieces; set aside.
2. Saute the onion, garlic and peppers in the drippings until tender, about 4 minutes. Add the diced tomatoes, lemon juice, basil, sugar, hot pepper sauce, bouillon, chili powder, pepper, thyme and 1 tsp. salt; cook and stir for 5 minutes. Add to the cooked rice. Stir in the ham, shrimp if desired, fresh parsley and sausage; mix lightly.
3. Just before baking, stuff chicken with about 3½ cups stuffing. Place remaining stuffing in a greased 1½-qt. baking dish; cover and refrigerate. Place chicken on a rack in a roasting pan; tie drumsticks together. Combine paprika, pepper and remaining salt; rub over chicken.
4. Bake, uncovered, at 350° for 1½ hours, basting every 30 minutes. Cover and bake 1½ hours longer or until juices run clear. Bake the additional stuffing for the last 40 minutes of baking time, uncovering during the last 10 minutes.
1 serving: 472 cal., 24g fat (6g sat. fat), 106mg chol., 766mg sod., 27g carb. (3g sugars, 2g fiber), 36g pro.

OVEN-ROASTED ASPARAGUS

OVEN-ROASTED ASPARAGUS

Asparagus never tasted so good! Simply seasoned with butter and green onions, they taste fresh and keep their bright green color, too. They're so good, you might want to make extra.
—Jody Fisher, Stewartstown, PA

Takes: 20 min. • **Makes:** 6 servings

- 2 lbs. fresh asparagus, trimmed
- ¼ cup butter, melted
- 2 to 4 green onions, chopped
- ½ tsp. salt

1. Preheat oven to 425°. Place the asparagus in a 15x10x1-in. pan. Toss with melted butter and chopped green onions; spread evenly. Sprinkle with the salt.
2. Roast until crisp-tender, 10-15 minutes.
1 serving: 87 cal., 8g fat (5g sat. fat), 20mg chol., 266mg sod., 4g carb. (1g sugars, 1g fiber), 2g pro.

"Excellent and quick way to prepare asparagus. I have made it without the onion, and I liked it that way, too."
—BSOMMER6, TASTEOFHOME.COM

SPECIAL RADICCHIO-SPINACH SALAD

You might not think the combo of mint, chipotle pepper and honey would play out, but get ready to be amazed! My spicy-sweet salad is simply delicious.
—Roxanne Chan, Albany, CA

Takes: 20 min. • **Makes:** 12 servings

- 6 cups fresh baby spinach
- 1 head radicchio, torn
- 2 cups fresh raspberries
- ½ cup raisins
- ¼ cup pine nuts, toasted
- ¼ cup thinly sliced red onion
- ¼ cup minced fresh mint
- 3 Tbsp. lime juice
- 2 Tbsp. olive oil
- 2 tsp. honey
- 1½ to 3 tsp. chopped chipotle pepper in adobo sauce
- ¼ tsp. salt
- ½ cup crumbled feta cheese

In a large salad bowl, combine the first 7 ingredients. In a small saucepan, combine the lime juice, oil, honey, chipotle pepper and salt. Cook and stir until blended and heated through. Immediately pour over salad; toss to coat. Sprinkle with cheese.
¾ cup: 92 cal., 5g fat (1g sat. fat), 3mg chol., 117mg sod., 11g carb. (6g sugars, 3g fiber), 3g pro. **Diabetic exchanges:** 1 vegetable, 1 fat, ½ fruit.

PERFECT DINNER ROLLS

PERFECT DINNER ROLLS

These rolls melt in your mouth. I loved them as a child, and I'm happy to make them for my kids because I know I am creating those same wonderful memories that my mom made for me!
—Gayleen Grote, Battleview, ND

Prep: 30 min. + rising • **Bake:** 15 min.
Makes: 2 dozen

- 1 Tbsp. active dry yeast
- 2¼ cups warm water (110° to 115°)
- ⅓ cup sugar
- ⅓ cup shortening
- ¼ cup powdered nondairy creamer
- 2¼ tsp. salt
- 6 to 7 cups bread flour

1. In a large bowl, dissolve yeast in warm water. Add the sugar, shortening, creamer, salt and 5 cups flour. Beat until smooth. Stir in enough remaining flour to form a soft dough (dough will be sticky).
2. Turn onto a floured surface; knead until smooth and elastic, 6-8 minutes. Place in a bowl coated with cooking spray, turning once to coat the top. Cover and let rise in a warm place until doubled, about 1 hour.
3. Punch dough down. Turn onto a lightly floured surface; divide into 24 pieces. Shape each into a roll. Place 2 in. apart on baking sheets coated with cooking spray. Cover and let rise until doubled, about 30 minutes.
4. Meanwhile, preheat the oven to 350°. Bake until lightly browned, 12-15 minutes. Remove from pans to wire racks.
1 roll: 142 cal., 3g fat (1g sat. fat), 0 chol., 222mg sod., 25g carb. (3g sugars, 1g fiber), 4g pro.

HONEY PEAR CHEESECAKE

We grow pear trees, so I'm always dabbling in pear desserts. Ginger gives this extra zing.
—Nancy Zimmerman,
Cape May Court House, NJ

Prep: 25 min. • **Bake:** 1½ hours + chilling
Makes: 12 servings

- 1½ cups crushed gingersnap cookies (about 30)
- ¼ cup sugar
- 4 to 6 Tbsp. butter, melted

FILLING

- 3 pkg. (8 oz. each) cream cheese, softened
- 1 cup honey, divided
- 1 Tbsp. lemon juice
- 2 tsp. minced fresh gingerroot
- 4 large eggs, room temperature, lightly beaten
- 3 peeled and chopped medium pears (about 1½ cups), divided
- ⅓ cup golden raisins
- 1 Tbsp. butter
- 1 cup chopped pecans, toasted

1. Preheat oven to 325°. Securely wrap a double thickness of heavy-duty foil (about 18 in. square) around and under a greased 9-in. springform pan. Combine crushed gingersnaps and sugar; stir in 4 Tbsp. butter, adding more as necessary. Press onto bottom and 1½ in. up sides of prepared pan.
2. Beat cream cheese until fluffy, gradually adding ⅔ cup honey, lemon juice and minced ginger. Add eggs; beat on low speed just until blended. Fold in 1 cup chopped pears and raisins. Pour into crust. Place springform pan in a larger baking pan; add 1 in. of hot water to larger pan. Bake until center is just set and the top appears dull, 1½-1¾ hours. Remove cheesecake from oven; remove springform from water bath.
3. Cool the cheesecake on a wire rack for 10 minutes. Loosen sides from pan with a knife; remove the foil. Cool 1 hour longer. Refrigerate overnight, covering when completely cooled. Remove rim from pan.
4. In a large skillet, melt butter over medium heat. Add remaining honey and pears; cook and stir until pears are tender. Stir in pecans. Top cake with pear-pecan mixture.

Note: To toast nuts, bake in a shallow pan in a 350° oven for 5-10 minutes or cook in a skillet over low heat until lightly browned, stirring occasionally.
1 slice: 552 cal., 36g fat (17g sat. fat), 142mg chol., 374mg sod., 54g carb. (40g sugars, 3g fiber), 8g pro.

TEST KITCHEN TIPS

For this cheesecake, try using honey with a mild flavor, such as orange blossom, clover or alfalfa honey. This will help the flavor of the pears shine through a bit more. Speaking of which, try Bartlett pears in this recipe. Their flavor is stronger than most other pears and can stand up to the other tastes in this homey dessert.

HONEY PEAR CHEESECAKE

**TRADITIONAL
MEAT LOAF**

TRADITIONAL MEAT LOAF

Homemade meat loaf is a must-have when it comes to comfort food. This version always freezes well, so I double the recipe and stash a loaf for a crazy day.
—Gail Graham, Maple Ridge, BC

Prep: 15 min. • **Bake:** 1 hour + standing
Makes: 6 servings

- 3 slices bread
- 1 large egg, lightly beaten
- ⅔ cup 2% milk
- 1 cup shredded cheddar cheese
- 1 medium onion, finely chopped
- ½ cup finely shredded carrot
- 1 tsp. salt
- ¼ tsp. pepper
- 1½ lbs. ground beef

GLAZE

- ¼ cup packed brown sugar
- ¼ cup ketchup
- 1 Tbsp. prepared mustard

1. Preheat oven to 350°. Tear bread into 2-in. pieces; place in a blender. Cover and pulse to form coarse crumbs; transfer to a large bowl. Stir in egg, milk, cheese, onion, carrot, salt and pepper. Add the beef; mix lightly but thoroughly. Transfer to a greased 9x5-in. loaf pan.
2. In a small bowl, mix the glaze ingredients; spread over the loaf. Bake 60-75 minutes or until a thermometer reads 160°. Let stand 10 minutes before slicing.

Freeze option: Bake meat loaf without glaze. Securely wrap cooled meat loaf in foil, then freeze. To use, partially thaw the meat loaf in refrigerator overnight. Prepare and spread glaze over top; reheat on a greased shallow baking pan in a preheated 350° oven until heated through and a thermometer inserted in center reads 165°.

1 slice: 394 cal., 21g fat (10g sat. fat), 128mg chol., 843mg sod., 23g carb. (15g sugars, 1g fiber), 28g pro.

Savory Meat Loaf: Omit shredded carrot. Saute ½ cup chopped green pepper with onion in 2 tsp. canola oil until tender. Add 2 minced garlic cloves and cook 1 minute. Cool slightly. Combine with the egg, milk, bread, cheese, salt and pepper. Add 1 tsp. crushed dried rosemary. Proceed as the recipe directs.

ROASTED VEGETABLES WITH SAGE

ROASTED VEGETABLES WITH SAGE

When I can't decide what veggie to serve, I simply roast a bunch. That's how we boost nutrition at our house.
Betty Fulks, Onia, AR

Prep: 20 min. • **Bake:** 35 min.
Makes: 8 servings

- 5 cups cubed peeled butternut squash
- ½ lb. fingerling potatoes (about 2 cups)
- 1 cup fresh Brussels sprouts, halved
- 1 cup fresh baby carrots
- 3 Tbsp. butter
- 1 Tbsp. minced fresh sage or 1 tsp. dried sage leaves
- 1 garlic clove, minced
- ½ tsp. salt

1. Preheat oven to 425°. Place vegetables in a large bowl. In a microwave, melt butter; stir in remaining ingredients. Add to vegetables and toss to coat.
2. Transfer to a greased 15x10x1-in. baking pan. Roast 35-45 minutes or until tender, stirring occasionally.

¾ cup: 122 cal., 5g fat (3g sat. fat), 11mg chol., 206mg sod., 20g carb. (4g sugars, 3g fiber), 2g pro. **Diabetic exchanges:** 1 starch, 1 fat.

FIVE-CHEESE RIGATONI

Who can resist cheesy pasta hot from the oven? This ooey-gooey rigatoni boasts a homemade creamy Swiss sauce that comes together in just a few minutes.
—Shirley Foltz, Dexter, KS

Prep: 25 min. • **Bake:** 25 min.
Makes: 9 servings

- 1 pkg. (16 oz.) rigatoni or large tube pasta
- 2 Tbsp. butter
- 3 Tbsp. all-purpose flour
- 1 tsp. salt
- ½ tsp. pepper
- 2½ cups whole milk
- ½ cup shredded Swiss cheese
- ½ cup shredded fontina cheese
- ½ cup shredded part-skim mozzarella cheese
- ½ cup grated Parmesan cheese, divided
- ½ cup grated Romano cheese, divided

1. Cook rigatoni according to the package directions.
2. Preheat oven to 375°. In a large saucepan, melt butter. Stir in the flour, salt and pepper until smooth. Gradually stir in milk; bring to a boil. Cook and stir 1-2 minutes or until thickened. Stir in Swiss, fontina, mozzarella, ¼ cup Parmesan and ¼ cup Romano cheese until melted.
3. Drain rigatoni; stir in the cheese sauce. Transfer to a greased 13x9-in. baking dish. Sprinkle with remaining Parmesan and Romano cheeses. Cover and bake for 20 minutes. Uncover; bake 5-10 minutes longer or until bubbly.

¾ cup: 362 cal., 14g fat (8g sat. fat), 40mg chol., 586mg sod., 42g carb. (5g sugars, 2g fiber), 18g pro.

TEST KITCHEN TIP

To keep pasta from sticking together when cooking, use a large pot with plenty of water. Add a little cooking oil if desired (this also prevents the water from boiling over).

FIVE-CHEESE RIGATONI

LEMON GINGER ICEBOX CAKE

Everyone searches for grand desserts that have easy ingredients and minimal effort. My icebox cake is the answer. It's a lifesaver when you need a no-fuss treat.
—Suzanne Banfield, Basking Ridge, NJ

Prep: 20 min. + chilling • **Makes:** 12 servings

- 1 pkg. (8 oz.) cream cheese, softened
- 2 tsp. grated lemon zest
- 1 jar (10 oz.) lemon curd
- 2 cups heavy whipping cream
- 2 pkg. (5¼ oz. each) thin ginger cookies
- 2 Tbsp. chopped crystallized ginger

1. In a large bowl, beat cream cheese and lemon zest until creamy. Beat in lemon curd until smooth. Gradually add cream, beating on medium-high speed until soft peaks form.
2. Line bottom of an 8-in. square dish with 9 cookies; spread with about ⅔ cup cream cheese mixture. Repeat the layers 6 times. Sprinkle with crystallized ginger. Refrigerate, covered, 2 hours or overnight.
Note: This recipe was tested with Anna's Ginger Thins Swedish cookies.
1 piece: 521 cal., 31g fat (19g sat. fat), 93mg chol., 340mg sod., 54g carb. (34g sugars, 0 fiber), 4g pro.

OLIVE & ONION QUICK BREAD

OLIVE & ONION QUICK BREAD

I've been baking for over 50 years, and I never get tired of trying new recipes for my family, friends and co-workers. Baking relaxes me. I feel like an artist creating a masterpiece of love. This savory loaf makes a great gift.
—Paula Marchesi, Lenhartsville, PA

Prep: 15 min. • **Bake:** 45 min. + cooling
Makes: 1 loaf (12 slices)

- 1 Tbsp. canola oil
- 1 medium onion, finely chopped
- 2 cups all-purpose flour
- 1 Tbsp. minced fresh rosemary
- 1 tsp. baking soda
- ½ tsp. salt
- 2 large eggs, room temperature
- 1 cup buttermilk
- 2 Tbsp. butter, melted
- ¼ cup plus 2 Tbsp. sharp cheddar cheese, divided
- ¼ cup each chopped pitted green and ripe olives

1. Preheat oven to 350°. In a skillet, heat oil over medium-high heat. Add onion; cook and stir until tender, 2-3 minutes. Remove from heat.
2. In a large bowl, whisk the flour, rosemary, baking soda and salt. In another bowl, whisk eggs, buttermilk and melted butter until blended. Add to flour mixture; stir just until moistened. Fold in ¼ cup cheese, chopped olives and onion.
3. Transfer to a greased 8x4-in. loaf pan. Bake 40 minutes. Sprinkle remaining cheese over top. Bake until a toothpick inserted in center comes out clean, 5-10 minutes longer. Cool in pan 10 minutes before removing to a wire rack to cool.
1 slice: 150 cal., 6g fat (2g sat. fat), 41mg chol., 373mg sod., 18g carb. (1g sugars, 1g fiber), 5g pro.

GRAMP'S
GERMAN-STYLE
POT ROAST

GRAMP'S GERMAN-STYLE POT ROAST

Grandpa was of German heritage and loved the old-world recipes given to him by his mother. I made a few changes to make this dish in the slow cooker and to give it a slightly updated flavor.
—Nancy Heishman, Las Vegas, NV

Prep: 20 min. • **Cook:** 6 hours + standing
Makes: 8 servings

- 4 thick-sliced bacon strips
- 1 lb. baby Yukon Gold potatoes
- 4 medium carrots, sliced
- 1 can (14 oz.) sauerkraut, rinsed and well drained
- ¾ cup chopped dill pickles
- 1 tsp. smoked paprika
- 1 tsp. ground allspice
- ½ tsp. kosher salt
- ½ tsp. pepper
- 1 boneless beef chuck roast (3 lbs.)
- 2 pkg. (14.40 oz. each) frozen pearl onions, thawed
- 4 garlic cloves, minced
- ½ cup stout beer or beef broth
- ⅓ cup Dusseldorf mustard
- ½ cup sour cream
- ½ cup minced fresh parsley

1. In a large skillet, cook bacon over medium heat until crisp. Carefully remove to paper towels to drain.
2. Meanwhile, place the potatoes, carrots, sauerkraut and pickles in a 7-qt. slow cooker. Mix paprika, allspice, salt and pepper, rub over roast. Brown roast in drippings over medium heat. Transfer to slow cooker. Add onions and garlic to drippings; cook and stir 1 minute. Stir in beer and mustard; pour over meat. Crumble bacon; add to slow cooker.
3. Cook, covered, on low until meat and vegetables are tender, 6-8 hours. Remove roast; let stand 10 minutes before slicing. Strain cooking juices. Reserve vegetables and juices; skim fat. Return the reserved vegetables and cooking juices to the slow cooker. Stir in sour cream; heat through. Serve with roast; sprinkle with parsley.
1 serving: 552 cal., 31g fat (12g sat. fat), 127mg chol., 926mg sod., 28g carb. (9g sugars, 6g fiber), 39g pro.

FLAKY BUTTERHORN ROLLS

FLAKY BUTTERHORN ROLLS

This dinner roll, slightly sweet and so very flaky, was my mother's recipe. It's simple to prepare because you don't need to have any kneading skills. My grandchildren have renamed them "Grandma's Croissants."
—Bernice Smith, Sturgeon Lake, MN

Prep: 30 min. + rising • **Bake:** 10 min./batch
Makes: 4 dozen

- 4 cups all-purpose flour
- ½ cup sugar
- 1 tsp. salt
- 1 cup cold butter, cubed, or shortening
- 1 pkg. (¼ oz.) active dry yeast
- ¼ cup warm water (110° to 115°)
- ¾ cup warm milk (110° to 115°)
- 1 large egg, room temperature, lightly beaten
- 4 Tbsp. butter, melted, divided

1. In a large bowl, combine the flour, sugar and salt. Cut in the cold butter until mixture resembles coarse crumbs. In another bowl, dissolve yeast in warm water; add to crumb mixture. Add milk and egg; mix well. Cover and refrigerate overnight.
2. Divide dough into 4 equal portions. On a lightly floured surface, roll 1 portion into a 12-in. circle. Brush with 1 Tbsp. melted butter; cut into 12 wedges.
3. Roll up, beginning with the wide end; place on greased baking sheets. Repeat with the remaining dough. Cover the dough and let rise in a warm place until nearly doubled, about 1 hour.
4. Bake at 375° for 10-12 minutes or until golden brown. Remove to wire racks.
1 roll: 92 cal., 5g fat (3g sat. fat), 18mg chol., 101mg sod., 10g carb. (2g sugars, 0 fiber), 1g pro.

MASHED CAULIFLOWER AU GRATIN

MASHED CAULIFLOWER AU GRATIN

Unless someone tells you, you might not know you're eating cauliflower. Even my grandchildren love this buttery, cheesy, creamy dish that tastes oh, so much like mashed potatoes.

—Sandie Parker, Elk Rapids, MI

Prep: 40 min. • **Cook:** 40 min.
Makes: 12 servings

- 2 large heads cauliflower, broken into florets
- 1½ cups shredded Parmesan cheese
- 1 cup shredded Colby-Monterey Jack cheese
- 6 Tbsp. butter, cubed
- ¾ tsp. garlic salt
- ½ tsp. Montreal steak seasoning

TOPPING
- 1 cup Italian-style panko (Japanese) bread crumbs
- ¼ cup butter, melted

1. Preheat oven to 350°. Place cauliflower in a stockpot; add water to cover. Bring to a boil. Reduce heat; simmer, uncovered, until very tender, 10-12 minutes. Drain; transfer to a large bowl. Mash cauliflower; stir in the cheeses, cubed butter and seasonings. Transfer to a greased 3-qt. or a 13x9-in. baking dish.

2. In a small bowl, mix bread crumbs and melted butter until evenly coated; sprinkle over cauliflower mixture. Bake, uncovered, until heated through and topping is golden brown, 40-50 minutes.

Freeze option: Cool unbaked casserole; cover and freeze. To use, partially thaw in refrigerator overnight. Remove from refrigerator 30 minutes before baking. Preheat oven to 350°. Bake casserole as directed, increasing time as necessary to heat through and for a thermometer inserted in center to read 165°.

¾ cup: 238 cal., 17g fat (10g sat. fat), 41mg chol., 612mg sod., 14g carb. (3g sugars, 4g fiber), 9g pro.

Swiss Mashed Cauliflower: Cook and mash cauliflower as directed. Add 1 cup shredded Swiss cheese, 2 Tbsp. butter, 1 tsp. salt, ½ tsp. pepper, ¼ tsp. garlic powder and ¼ to ⅓ cup 2% milk.

NOTHING BUT THE BEST
When purchasing fresh heads of cauliflower, look for compact florets that are free from yellow or brown spots. The leaves should be crisp and green, not withered or discolored.

DATE-NUT PINWHEELS

Pinwheel cookies with dates and walnuts are a longtime family treasure. There are a few steps when prepping, so I sometimes freeze the dough and bake later.
—Frieda Whiteley, Lisbon, CT

- -

Prep: 30 min. + chilling • **Bake:** 10 min./batch
Makes: about 9 dozen

- 1   cup butter, softened
- 1   cup sugar
- 1   cup packed brown sugar
- 2   large eggs, room temperature
- 4   cups all-purpose flour
- ½   tsp. baking soda

FILLING
- 2   pkg. (8 oz. each) pitted dates
- 1   cup water
- ½   cup sugar
- ½   cup chopped walnuts

1. In a large bowl, cream butter and sugars until light and fluffy. Beat in eggs. In another bowl, whisk flour and baking soda; gradually beat into creamed mixture. Divide the dough into 3 portions. Shape each portion into a disk. Cover and refrigerate for 1 hour or until firm enough to roll.

2. For filling, place dates, water and sugar in a large saucepan. Bring to a boil. Reduce heat; simmer, uncovered, until dates are tender and liquid is almost evaporated. Stir in walnuts; cool completely.

3. Roll each portion between 2 sheets of waxed paper into a 12x10-in. rectangle. Refrigerate 30 minutes. Remove the waxed paper. Spread a third of the filling over each rectangle. Roll up tightly jelly-roll style, starting with a long side. Wrap securely. Refrigerate until firm.

4. Preheat oven to 350°. Unwrap and cut dough crosswise into ⅓-in. slices. Place 2 in. apart on greased baking sheets. Bake for 10-12 minutes or until set. Remove from pans to wire racks to cool.

1 cookie: 67 cal., 2g fat (1g sat. fat), 8mg chol., 21mg sod., 12g carb. (7g sugars, 1g fiber), 1g pro.

DATE-NUT PINWHEELS

HONEY COFFEE

For a soothing pick-me-up, sip on this pleasantly sweet coffee. Give it a try, and it is sure to become a new favorite in your home today.
—*Taste of Home* Test Kitchen

- -

Takes: 10 min. • **Makes:** 4 servings

- 2   cups hot strong brewed coffee (French or other dark roast)
- ½   cup whole milk
- ¼   cup honey
- ⅛   tsp. ground cinnamon
      Dash ground nutmeg
- ¼   tsp. vanilla extract

In a small saucepan, combine the coffee, milk, honey, cinnamon and nutmeg. Cook and stir until heated through. (Do not boil.) Remove from the heat; stir in vanilla. Pour into cups or mugs; serve immediately.

½ cup: 86 cal., 1g fat (1g sat. fat), 4mg chol., 18mg sod., 19g carb. (18g sugars, 0 fiber), 1g pro.

MENU
SPRING SUPPER

BOURBON-SPICED
GLAZED HAM

BOURBON-SPICED GLAZED HAM

This bourbon-spiked ham makes a wonderful main course for a holiday feast. Leftovers (if there are any) make delicious sandwiches.
—Karen Sublett-Young, Princeton, IN

Prep: 20 min. + marinating • **Bake:** 3 hours
Makes: 16 servings

    7 to 9 lbs. fully cooked bone-in ham
    1 cup packed brown sugar
    1 cup orange juice
    1 cup bourbon
 1½ tsp. ground cloves

1. Place ham in a large resealable plastic bag. Whisk together remaining ingredients until blended; pour into bag. Seal bag and turn to coat. Refrigerate 8 hours or overnight.
2. Preheat oven to 325°. Remove ham from marinade and place on a rack in a roasting pan; reserve remaining marinade, placing it in the refrigerator until ready to baste.
3. Using a sharp knife, score surface of ham with ¼-in.-deep cuts in a diamond pattern. Bake, covered, 2 hours.
4. Baste with roughly half of the reserved marinade. Bake, uncovered, 1-1½ hours, basting the ham 2 more times during the first half hour, until a thermometer reads 140°.
4 oz. cooked ham: 182 cal., 5g fat (2g sat. fat), 87mg chol., 1,042mg sod., 4g carb. (3g sugars, 0 fiber), 29g pro.

WARM FAVA BEAN & PEA SALAD

This is a springtime staple in my house; my mom has been making it forever. I know that when the favas are at the market I can always find this refreshing and tasty salad in her fridge! If fresh favas or peas are not available, frozen is fine — but if you use frozen favas, be sure to take off the tough outer skin first.
—Francesca Ferenczi, New York, NY

Prep: 55 min. • **Cook:** 25 min.
Makes: 12 servings

    3 cups shelled fresh fava beans
       (about 4 lbs. unshelled) or 1 pkg.
       (28 oz.) frozen fava beans, thawed
    8 cups shelled fresh peas (about
       8 lbs. unshelled) or 8 cups
       frozen peas (about 32 oz.)
    3 Tbsp. olive oil, divided
    4 oz. diced pancetta
    8 shallots, thinly sliced
  ½ tsp. salt
  ¼ tsp. pepper

WARM FAVA BEAN & PEA SALAD

1. For fresh fava beans, add beans to a large pot of boiling water; return to a boil. Cook, uncovered, until tender, 4-5 minutes. Using a strainer, remove beans to a bowl of ice water to cool. Drain cooled beans; squeeze gently to remove skins. (If using frozen fava beans, prepare according to package directions.)
2. For fresh peas, add peas to boiling water; return to a boil. Cook, uncovered, just until tender, 2-4 minutes. Drain well; place in a large bowl. (If using frozen peas, cook according to package directions.)
3. In a large skillet, heat 1 Tbsp. oil over medium heat. Add pancetta; cook and stir until crisp, about 5 minutes. Drain on paper towels, reserving drippings.
4. In same pan, heat remaining oil and reserved drippings over medium heat. Add shallots; cook and stir until tender and lightly browned, 5-6 minutes. Stir in fava beans and heat through. Add to peas; stir in salt, pepper and pancetta. Serve warm.
Note: Three cups frozen shelled edamame may be substituted for fava beans; prepare according to package directions.
¾ cup: 293 cal., 7g fat (2g sat. fat), 8mg chol., 282mg sod., 49g carb. (35g sugars, 8g fiber), 10g pro.

EASY BISCUIT MUFFINS

These simple biscuits are made with readily available ingredients—you'd never know there's mayonnaise in them! If you adapt this recipe for jumbo-sized muffin tins, be sure to give them a little more baking time.
—Taryn Ellis, Wyoming, MI

- -

Prep: 10 min. • **Bake:** 25 min.
Makes: 1 dozen

3	cups all-purpose flour
4	tsp. baking powder
1½	tsp. sugar
1	tsp. salt
1½	cups whole milk
½	cup mayonnaise

1. Preheat oven to 350°. Whisk together first 4 ingredients. In another bowl, whisk milk and mayonnaise until blended; add to dry ingredients, stirring just until moistened (batter will be thick).
2. Spoon ¼ cup of the mixture into each of 12 greased or paper-lined muffin cups. Bake until golden brown, 25-30 minutes. Cool 5 minutes before removing from pan to a wire rack. Serve warm.
1 muffin: 194 cal., 8g fat (2g sat. fat), 4mg chol., 417mg sod., 26g carb. (2g sugars, 1g fiber), 4g pro.

BUTTERY CARROTS

My mother made this recipe often when I was growing up. She got it from a friend who was a chef at a local restaurant my parents frequented. The onions really bring out the sweetness of the carrots. When I have carrots fresh from the garden, I don't even peel them—I just scrub them well before cutting. For large buffets, I often double or triple this recipe
—Mary Ellen Chambers, Lakewood, OH

- -

Takes: 20 min.
Makes: 12 servings

3	lbs. medium carrots, halved crosswise and cut into strips
2	medium onions, halved and thinly sliced
½	cup butter, melted
½	cup chopped fresh parsley
½	tsp. salt
	Coarsely ground pepper, optional

1. Place 2 in. of water in a 6-qt. stockpot. Add carrots and onions; bring to a boil. Reduce heat; simmer, covered, until the carrots are crisp-tender, 10-12 minutes.
2. Drain the vegetables. Toss with the remaining ingredients.
¾ cup: 123 cal., 8g fat (5g sat. fat), 20mg chol., 240mg sod., 13g carb. (6g sugars, 4g fiber), 1g pro.

EASY BISCUIT MUFFINS

STRAWBERRY
SHORTCAKE
PUFFS

STRAWBERRY SHORTCAKE PUFFS

When my wonderful friend Kelly brought me a pint of strawberries, I didn't want to just eat them straight (tempting as it was). I decided to make strawberry shortcake with my own pretty, elegant spin. These light and airy puff pastry stacks let the fruit shine.
—Jenny Dubinsky, Inwood, WV

Prep: 25 min. • **Bake:** 15 min. + cooling
Makes: 12 servings

- 1 sheet frozen puff pastry, thawed
- 4 cups fresh strawberries, sliced
- ¼ cup plus 3 Tbsp. sugar, divided
- 1½ cups heavy whipping cream
- ½ tsp. vanilla extract

1. Preheat oven to 400°. On a lightly floured surface, roll puff pastry to a 10-in. square; cut into 12 rectangles (approx. 3x2½ in.). Place on ungreased baking sheets. Bake until golden brown, 12-15 minutes. Remove to wire racks; cool completely.
2. In a large bowl, toss the strawberries with ¼ cup sugar. Let stand 30 minutes, stirring occasionally. In another bowl, beat cream until it begins to thicken. Add the vanilla and remaining sugar; beat until stiff peaks form.
3. To serve, split pastries horizontally in half. Top each bottom half with 2 Tbsp. whipped cream and 1 Tbsp. strawberries; replace top half. Top with the remaining whipped cream and strawberries.

1 serving: 246 cal., 16g fat (8g sat. fat), 34mg chol., 76mg sod., 23g carb. (11g sugars, 2g fiber), 3g pro.

TEST KITCHEN TIP
Save time when you prepare the strawberries and the whipped cream a day ahead of time. Store it all in the fridge until you're ready to bake the puff pastry. Once the pastry cools, you can simply assemble and serve the colorful treats.

GRANDMA'S FAVORITE
COOKIES, BROWNIE'S & BARS

Grandma's cookie jar was always full of yummy home-baked treats. Turn here whenever you need a sweet escape, a bite to share, or a delicious remembrance of simple, happy times.

FROSTED OATMEAL COOKIES

A woman in my Iowa hometown sold these cookies. When my grandmother asked her for the recipe, she agreed—as long as my grandmother promised not to make them until the woman had grown too old to sell them. Grandmother kept her promise, and this special recipe has been a family favorite for many years.
—Bonnie Capper-Eckstein, Osseo, MN

- -

Prep: 45 min. + chilling
Bake: 10 min./batch + cooling
Makes: about 4 dozen

- 1   cup butter, softened
- 2   cups packed brown sugar
- 2   large eggs, room temperature
- 2   cups all-purpose flour
- 2   cups quick-cooking oats
- 1   tsp. baking soda
- 1   tsp. salt
- 1   tsp. ground allspice
- 1   tsp. ground cinnamon
- ¼   tsp. ground cloves
- 1   cup raisins
- 1   cup chopped pecans, optional

FROSTING
- 5   cups confectioners' sugar
- ¼   cup butter, melted
- ⅓   to ½ cup 2% milk
     White sprinkles, optional

1. Cream butter and brown sugar until light and fluffy. Beat in eggs. In another bowl, whisk next 7 ingredients; gradually beat into creamed mixture. Stir in raisins and, if desired, pecans. Divide dough in half. Shape each into a disk; cover. Refrigerate until firm enough to roll, about 1 hour.
2. Preheat oven to 350°. On a lightly floured surface, roll each portion of dough to ¼-in. thickness. Cut with a floured 2¾-in. round cookie cutter. Place 2 in. apart on greased baking sheets. Bake until light brown, 7-9 minutes. Cool 2 minutes before removing from pans to wire racks to cool completely.
3. For frosting, beat confectioners' sugar, butter and enough milk to reach spreading consistency. Spread over cookies. If desired, top with white sprinkles.
1 cookie: 164 cal., 5g fat (3g sat. fat), 20mg chol., 116mg sod., 29g carb. (22g sugars, 1g fiber), 1g pro.

WINNING APRICOT BARS

This recipe is down-home baking at its best, and it really represents all regions of the country. It's won blue ribbons at county fairs and cookie contests in several states! This treat is easy to make, and it's perfect for potluck suppers, bake sales, lunchboxes or just plain snacking.
—Jill Moritz, Irvine, CA

- -

Prep: 15 min. • **Bake:** 30 min. + cooling
Makes: 2 dozen

- ¾   cup butter, softened
- 1   cup sugar
- 1   large egg, room temperature
- ½   tsp. vanilla extract
- 2   cups all-purpose flour
- ¼   tsp. baking powder
- 1⅓ cups sweetened shredded coconut
- ½   cup chopped walnuts
- 1   jar (10 to 12 oz.) apricot preserves

1. Preheat oven to 350°. In a large bowl, cream butter and sugar until light and fluffy. Beat in egg and vanilla. In a small bowl, whisk flour and baking powder; gradually add to creamed mixture, mixing well. Fold in the coconut and walnuts.
2. Press two-thirds of dough onto the bottom of a greased 13x9-in. baking pan. Spread with preserves; crumble remaining dough over preserves. Bake 30-35 minutes or until golden brown. Cool completely in pan on a wire rack. Cut into bars.
1 bar: 195 cal., 10g fat (6g sat. fat), 23mg chol., 72mg sod., 27g carb. (16g sugars, 1g fiber), 2g pro.

> "These bars are so easy. They are very good any time of year. I tried using other flavors of jam, like raspberry, which was also very good."
> —COOKIECORNER, TASTEOFHOME.COM

FROSTED OATMEAL COOKIES

WINNING
APRICOT BARS

MINCEMEAT COOKIE BARS

My daughter won the grand champion title at the Alaska State Fair with these bars when she was 10. The topping is delicious but a bit crumbly; for neatly edged cookies, freeze them before cutting.
—Mary Bohanan, Sparks, NV

Prep: 15 min. • **Bake:** 30 min. + cooling
Makes: 3 dozen

- 1 tsp. butter
- 2 cups all-purpose flour
- 1 cup sugar
- ½ tsp. baking soda
- ½ tsp. salt
- ½ cup canola oil
- ¼ cup 2% milk
- 1 jar (28 oz.) prepared mincemeat
- 1 cup chopped pecans

1. Preheat oven to 400°. Line an 8-in. square baking pan with foil; grease foil with butter. In a large bowl, whisk flour, sugar, baking soda and salt. Stir in oil and milk. Reserve 1 cup for topping. Press remaining crumb mixture onto bottom of prepared pan. Spread with mincemeat. Stir pecans into reserved crumb mixture; sprinkle over the top. Bake 30-35 minutes or until topping is golden brown.
2. Cool completely in pan on a wire rack. Cut into bars.
1 bar: 134 cal., 6g fat (1g sat. fat), 0 chol., 59mg sod., 20g carb. (13g sugars, 1g fiber), 1g pro.

GINGERBREAD MERINGUE BARS

GINGERBREAD MERINGUE BARS

For the best of both worlds, I combined my grandmother's gingerbread recipe with my aunt's special brown sugar meringue. The result? These lovable holiday-perfect bars.
—Eden Dranger, Los Angeles, CA

Prep: 20 min. • **Bake:** 30 min. + cooling
Makes: 2 dozen

- ¼ cup butter, softened
- 1 cup molasses
- 2 large egg yolks, room temperature
- 1 large egg, room temperature
- ¼ cup canned pumpkin
- 1 tsp. vanilla extract
- 1½ cups whole wheat flour
- 2½ tsp. ground cinnamon
- 2 tsp. ground ginger
- 1 tsp. baking powder
- 1 tsp. baking soda
- ¾ tsp. ground allspice
- ¼ tsp. salt
- 1 cup miniature marshmallows
- ½ cup chopped pecans
- ½ cup semisweet chocolate chips

MERINGUE
- 4 large egg whites, room temperature
- ½ cup packed brown sugar

1. In a large bowl, beat butter and molasses until blended. Add egg yolks and egg, one at a time, beating well after each addition. Beat in pumpkin and vanilla.
2. In a small bowl, combine the flour, cinnamon, ginger, baking powder, baking soda, allspice and salt. Gradually add to the molasses mixture. Pour into a greased 13x9-in. baking pan. Sprinkle with marshmallows, pecans and chocolate chips. Bake at 350° for 20 minutes.
3. Meanwhile, in a small bowl, beat egg whites on medium speed until soft peaks form. Gradually beat in brown sugar, 1 Tbsp. at a time, on high until stiff glossy peaks form and sugar is dissolved.
4. Remove gingerbread from oven; spread with meringue. Bake until meringue is lightly browned, 9-11 minutes. Cool completely. Cut into bars.
1 bar: 135 cal., 4g fat (2g sat. fat), 31mg chol., 129mg sod., 24g carb. (15g sugars, 1g fiber), 2g pro. **Diabetic exchanges:** 1½ starch, 1 fat.

BLACKBERRY PEEKABOO COOKIES

My grandmother bakes this recipe every year for the holidays. She uses homemade blackberry jam that she makes fresh every summer. The cookies are so delicious!
—Jacquie Franklin, Hot Springs, MT

- -

Prep: 15 min. + chilling
Bake: 10 min./batch + cooling
Makes: about 3 dozen

- ½ cup butter, softened
- ½ cup shortening
- 2 cups packed brown sugar
- 2 large eggs, room temperature
- 1 tsp. vanilla extract
- 4 cups all-purpose flour
- 1½ tsp. baking soda
- 1½ tsp. salt
- ¾ cup seedless blackberry spreadable fruit

1. Cream butter, shortening and brown sugar until light and fluffy. Add 1 egg at a time, beating well after each addition. Beat in vanilla. In another bowl, whisk flour, baking soda and salt; gradually beat into creamed mixture. Divide dough in half. Shape each into a disk; cover. Refrigerate until firm enough to roll, about 30 minutes.

2. Preheat oven to 350°. On a lightly floured surface, roll each portion of dough to ⅛-in. thickness. Cut with a floured 2-in. round cookie cutter. Place half of the circles onto parchment-lined baking sheets. Spread 1 tsp. spreadable fruit in the center of each circle; top with remaining circles, pressing edges lightly to seal.

3. Bake until light brown, 10-12 minutes. Remove from pans to wire racks to cool.

1 cookie: 162 cal., 6g fat (2g sat. fat), 17mg chol., 179mg sod., 26g carb. (15g sugars, 0 fiber), 2g pro.

CHOCOLATE-COCONUT LAYER BARS

I'm a huge fan of Nanaimo bars, the no-bake layered dessert named for the city in British Columbia. For fun, I reinvented this treat with coconut lovers in mind.
—Shannon Dobos, Calgary, AB

- -

Prep: 20 min. + chilling • **Makes:** 3 dozen

- ¾ cup butter, cubed
- 3 cups Oreo cookie crumbs
- 2 cups sweetened shredded coconut
- ½ cup cream of coconut

FILLING
- ⅓ cup butter, softened
- 3 Tbsp. cream of coconut
- ¼ tsp. coconut extract
- 3 cups confectioners' sugar
- 1 to 2 Tbsp. 2% milk

TOPPING
- 1½ cups semisweet chocolate chips
- 4 tsp. canola oil
- 3 Mounds candy bars (1¾ oz. each), coarsely chopped, optional

1. Microwave butter on high until melted; stir until smooth. Stir in cookie crumbs, coconut and cream of coconut until blended (mixture will be wet). Spread onto bottom of an ungreased 13x9-in. baking pan. Refrigerate until set, about 30 minutes.

2. For filling, beat butter, cream of coconut and extract until smooth. Gradually beat in confectioners' sugar and enough milk to reach a spreading consistency. Spread over the crust.

3. For topping, microwave chocolate chips and oil until melted; stir until smooth. Cool slightly; spread over filling. If desired, sprinkle with chopped candy bars. Refrigerate.

1 bar: 229 cal., 13g fat (8g sat. fat), 15mg chol., 124mg sod., 28g carb. (23g sugars, 1g fiber), 1g pro.

BLACKBERRY PEEKABOO COOKIES

SWEET POTATO CHEESECAKE BARS

Your house will be filled with the aroma of pumpkin spice when you bake these bars. They look complicated, but are so easy that you can whip up a batch anytime. A cake mix makes it simple.
—Nancy Whitford, Edwards, NY

- -

Prep: 20 min. • **Bake:** 25 min. + chilling
Makes: 2 dozen

- 1 pkg. yellow cake mix (regular size)
- ½ cup butter, softened
- 1 large egg, room temperature

FILLING
- 1 can (15 oz.) sweet potatoes, drained
- 1 pkg. (8 oz.) cream cheese, cubed
- ½ cup plus ¼ cup sugar, divided
- 1 large egg
- 1½ tsp. pumpkin pie spice
- 1 cup sour cream
- ¼ tsp. vanilla extract

TOPPING
- 1¼ cups granola without raisins
- ½ cup white baking chips
- ¼ tsp. pumpkin pie spice

1. In a large bowl, beat the cake mix, butter and egg until crumbly. Press onto the bottom of a greased 13x9-in. baking dish.
2. Place the sweet potatoes, cream cheese, ½ cup sugar, egg and pie spice in a food processor; cover and process until blended. Spread over crust.
3. Bake at 350° until center is almost set, 20-25 minutes. Meanwhile, in a small bowl, combine the sour cream, vanilla and remaining sugar. Spread over filling.
4. Combine topping ingredients; sprinkle over top. Bake just until set, 5-8 minutes longer. Cool on a wire rack.
5. Refrigerate 2 hours. Cut into bars.
1 bar: 259 cal., 13g fat (7g sat. fat), 45mg chol., 217mg sod., 34g carb. (22g sugars, 2g fiber), 4g pro.

CHEWY CHOCOLATE COOKIES

This cookie recipe—a favorite of our four children—has been in my collection for years. Sometimes I substitute mint-flavored chips for the semisweet chocolate ones. Either way, the cookies always seem to disappear fast.
—Sheri Ziesemer, Olympia, WA

- -

Prep: 20 min. • **Bake:** 10 min./batch
Makes: about 4½ dozen

- 1¼ cups butter, softened
- 2 cups sugar
- 2 large eggs, room temperature
- 2 tsp. vanilla extract
- 2 cups all-purpose flour
- ¾ cup baking cocoa
- 1 tsp. baking soda
- ½ tsp. salt
- 2 cups (12 oz.) semisweet chocolate chips

1. Preheat oven to 350°. In a large bowl, cream butter and sugar until light and fluffy. Beat in eggs and vanilla. In another bowl, whisk flour, cocoa, baking soda and salt; gradually add to creamed mixture. Stir in the chips.
2. Drop by teaspoonfuls onto lightly greased baking sheets. Bake 8-10 minutes (do not overbake). Cool on pans 1 minute. Remove to wire racks to cool.
2 cookies: 238 cal., 13 g fat (8 g sat. fat), 38 mg chol., 182 mg sod., 31 g carb., 1 g fiber, 2 g pro.

SWEET POTATO CHEESECAKE BARS

SWEDISH ALMOND RUSKS

Not too sweet, these nutty, crunchy cookies go well with a cup of hot coffee...and travel well in care packages, too!
—Judy Videen, Moorehead, MN

Prep: 20 min. • **Bake:** 40 min.
Makes: 6 dozen

- 1 cup butter, softened
- 1¾ cups sugar
- 2 large eggs, room temperature
- 2 tsp. almond extract
- 5 cups all-purpose flour
- 1 tsp. ground cardamom
- 1 tsp. baking soda
- 1 cup sour cream
- 1 cup finely chopped almonds

In a bowl, cream butter and sugar. Add 1 egg at a time, beating well after each addition. Stir in extract. Sift together flour, cardamom and soda; add alternately with sour cream to creamed mixture. Fold in almonds. Divide dough into 6 parts; shape into rolls (like refrigerated cookie dough). Place 3 each on 2 greased baking sheets. Bake at 350° for about 30 minutes or until light brown. Remove rolls to cutting board. Using a sharp knife, slice rolls diagonally ½ in. thick. Place cookies on sheets; return to oven and bake until light brown. Cool; store in tightly covered containers.

2 rusks: 184 cal., 8g fat (4g sat. fat), 30mg chol., 93mg sod., 24g carb. (10g sugars, 1g fiber), 3g pro.

GREAT-GRANDMA'S
OATMEAL COOKIES

GREAT-GRANDMA'S OATMEAL COOKIES

This recipe, a real favorite of my husband's, goes back to my great-grandmother. At Christmastime, we use colored sugar for a festive touch.
—Mary Ann Konechne, Kimball, SD

Prep: 35 min. • **Bake:** 15 min./batch + cooling
Makes: about 12 dozen

- 1½ cups shortening
- 2 cups sugar
- 4 large eggs, room temperature
- 4 tsp. water
- 4 cups all-purpose flour
- 2 tsp. baking soda
- 2 tsp. ground cinnamon
- ½ tsp. salt
- 4 cups quick-cooking oats
- 2 cups chopped raisins
- 1 cup chopped walnuts
  Additional sugar or colored sugar

1. Preheat oven to 350°. Cream shortening and sugar until light and fluffy. Add 1 egg at a time, beating well after each addition. Beat in water. In another bowl, whisk together flour, baking soda, cinnamon and salt; add to creamed mixture, and mix well. Stir in oats, raisins and walnuts.

2. On a surface sprinkled with additional granulated or colored sugar, roll dough to ¼-in. thickness. Cut with a floured 2½-in. cookie cutter in desired shapes. Place 2 in. apart on greased baking sheets. Bake until set, 12-15 minutes. Remove to wire racks to cool.

1 cookie: 63 cal., 3g fat (1g sat. fat), 5mg chol., 28mg sod., 9g carb. (4g sugars, 0 fiber), 1g pro.

TEST KITCHEN TIP

If you want to add a finishing touch to these cookies, mix 1 cup confectioners' sugar with ¼ tsp. cinnamon and 5-6 tsp. water to make a quick glaze.

CHRISTMAS CUTOUTS

Making and decorating these tender sugar cookies left a lasting impression on our four children. Now that they're grown, they've all asked for my recipe, baking memories with their own children.
—Shirley Kidd, New London, MN

Prep: 25 min. + chilling
Bake: 10 min/batch + cooling
Makes: about 3½ dozen

- 1 cup butter, softened
- 1½ cups confectioners' sugar
- 1 large egg, room temperature
- 1 tsp. vanilla extract
- ½ tsp. almond extract
- 2½ cups all-purpose flour
- 1 tsp. baking soda
- 1 tsp. cream of tartar

FROSTING
- 3¾ cups confectioners' sugar
- 3 Tbsp. butter, softened
- 1 tsp. vanilla extract
- 2 to 4 Tbsp. 2% milk
  Liquid or paste food coloring and assorted sprinkles, optional

1. Cream butter and confectioners' sugar until light and fluffy. Beat in egg and extracts. In another bowl, whisk together flour, baking soda and cream of tartar; gradually beat into creamed mixture. Shape into a disk; wrap in plastic. Refrigerate until firm enough to roll, 2-3 hours.
2. Preheat oven to 375°. On a lightly floured surface, roll dough to ⅛-in. thickness. Cut with floured 2-in. cookie cutters. Place on ungreased baking sheets.
3. Bake until edges begin to brown, 7-8 minutes. Remove from pan to wire racks; cool completely.
4. For frosting, beat the confectioners' sugar, butter, vanilla and enough milk to reach desired consistency; tint with food coloring if desired. Spread over cookies. Decorate as desired.
1 cookie: 134 cal., 5g fat (3g sat. fat), 18mg chol., 74mg sod., 21g carb. (15g sugars, 0 fiber), 1g pro.

PEPPERMINT BROWNIES

PEPPERMINT BROWNIES

My grandmother encouraged me to enter these mint brownies in the county fair some years ago—and they earned top honors. They're a great chewy treat to serve during the holidays.
—Marcy Greenblatt, Redding, CA

Prep: 15 min. • **Bake:** 35 min.
Makes: 2 dozen

- 1⅓ cups all-purpose flour
- 1 cup baking cocoa
- 1 tsp. salt
- 1 tsp. baking powder
- ¾ cup canola oil
- 2 cups sugar
- 2 tsp. vanilla extract
- 4 large eggs
- ⅔ cup crushed peppermint candies

GLAZE
- 1 cup (6 oz.) semisweet chocolate chips
- 1 Tbsp. shortening
- 2 Tbsp. crushed peppermint candies

1. Preheat oven to 350°. Line a 13x9-in. baking pan with foil; grease foil.
2. In a bowl, whisk together first 4 ingredients. In a large bowl, beat oil and sugar until blended. Beat in vanilla and eggs, one at a time, beating well after each addition. Gradually add flour mixture; stir in crushed peppermint candies. Spread into prepared pan.
3. Bake until a toothpick inserted in center comes out clean, 35-40 minutes. Cool in pan on a wire rack.
4. In a microwave, melt chocolate chips and shortening; stir until smooth. Spread over brownies; sprinkle with candies.
1 brownie: 222 cal., 11g fat (3g sat. fat), 35mg chol., 128mg sod., 31g carb. (22g sugars, 1g fiber), 3g pro.

GRANDMA'S FAVORITE
CAKES & PIES

A slice of Grandma's from-scratch dessert is like a big warm hug just when you need it most. Relish every last bite of these heavenly treats that always make the day just a tiny bit brighter.

SUGAR CREAM PIE

SUGAR CREAM PIE

I absolutely love creamy sugar pie, especially the one that my grandma made for me. We serve it warm or chilled.
—Laura Kipper, Westfield, IN

- -

Prep: 20 min. • **Bake:** 15 min. + chilling
Makes: 8 servings

Pastry for single-crust pie (9 in.)
1 cup sugar
¼ cup cornstarch
2 cups 2% milk
½ cup butter, cubed
1 tsp. vanilla extract
¼ tsp. ground cinnamon

1. Preheat oven to 450°. Roll out dough to fit a 9-in. pie plate. Transfer crust to pie plate. Trim crust to ½ in. beyond rim of plate; flute edge. Line unpricked crust with a double thickness of heavy-duty foil. Fill with pie weights, dried beans or uncooked rice.
2. Bake for 8 minutes. Remove foil and weights; bake 5-7 minutes longer or until light brown. Cool on a wire rack. Reduce oven setting to 375°.
3. Meanwhile, in a large saucepan, combine the sugar and cornstarch; stir in milk until smooth. Bring to a boil. Reduce heat; cook and stir 2 minutes or until thickened and bubbly. Remove from heat; stir in butter and vanilla. Transfer to crust; sprinkle with cinnamon. Bake 15-20 minutes or until golden brown. Cool the pie on a wire rack; refrigerate until chilled.
1 piece: 418 cal., 24g fat (15g sat. fat), 66mg chol., 275mg sod., 47g carb. (28g sugars, 1g fiber), 4g pro.

> ### TEST KITCHEN TIP
> For a fun change of pace, try baking this pie in a crumb crust. Graham crackers, gingersnaps and vanilla wafer cookies all work well and taste delicious.

ZUCCHINI CUPCAKES

I asked my grandmother for this recipe after trying these irresistible spice cupcakes at her home. I love their creamy caramel frosting. They're such a scrumptious dessert, you actually forget you're eating your vegetables, too!
—Virginia Lapierre, Greensboro Bend, VT

- -

Prep: 20 min. • **Bake:** 20 min. + cooling
Makes: about 1½ dozen

3 large eggs, room temperature
1⅓ cups sugar
½ cup canola oil
½ cup orange juice
1 tsp. almond extract
2½ cups all-purpose flour
2 tsp. ground cinnamon
2 tsp. baking powder
1 tsp. baking soda
1 tsp. salt
½ tsp. ground cloves
1½ cups shredded zucchini

ZUCCHINI CUPCAKES

FROSTING
1 cup packed brown sugar
½ cup butter, cubed
¼ cup 2% milk
1 tsp. vanilla extract
1½ to 2 cups confectioners' sugar

1. Preheat oven to 350°. Beat the first 5 ingredients. Combine dry ingredients; gradually add to egg mixture and blend well. Stir in zucchini.
2. Fill paper-lined muffin cups two-thirds full. Bake until a toothpick inserted in center comes out clean, 20-25 minutes. Cool for 10 minutes before removing to a wire rack.
3. For frosting, combine the brown sugar, butter and milk in a large saucepan. Bring to a boil over medium heat; cook and stir until thickened, 1-2 minutes. Remove from heat; stir in vanilla. Cool to lukewarm.
4. Gradually beat in the confectioners' sugar until frosting reaches spreading consistency. Frost cupcakes.
1 cupcake: 327 cal., 12g fat (4g sat. fat), 45mg chol., 305mg sod., 52g carb. (38g sugars, 1g fiber), 3g pro.

FAVORITE DUTCH APPLE PIE

Everything about this dessert makes it the top request for family get-togethers. The delightful crust cuts beautifully to reveal a filling of diced apple. At harvesttime or any time, you cannot beat this delectable pie.
—Brenda DuFresne, Midland, MI

Prep: 20 min. • **Bake:** 40 min. + cooling
Makes: 8 servings

- 2 cups all-purpose flour
- 1 cup packed brown sugar
- ½ cup quick-cooking oats
- ¾ cup butter, melted

FILLING
- ⅔ cup sugar
- 3 Tbsp. cornstarch
- 1¼ cups cold water
- 4 cups chopped peeled tart apples (about 2 large)
- 1 tsp. vanilla extract

1. Preheat oven to 350°. Mix flour, brown sugar, oats and butter; reserve 1½ cups mixture for topping. Press remaining mixture onto bottom and up sides of an ungreased 9-in. pie plate.
2. In a large saucepan, mix sugar, cornstarch and water until smooth; bring to a boil. Cook and stir until thickened, about 2 minutes. Remove from heat; stir in apples and vanilla. Pour into crust. Crumble topping over filling.
3. Bake until the crust is golden brown and the filling is bubbly, 40-45 minutes. Cool pie on a wire rack.

1 piece: 494 cal., 18g fat (11g sat. fat), 46mg chol., 146mg sod., 81g carb. (49g sugars, 2g fiber), 4g pro.

GLAZED CHOCOLATE ANGEL FOOD CAKE

GLAZED CHOCOLATE ANGEL FOOD CAKE

It's OK to lose track of how many slices of this delightful cake you eat. Light as air and loaded with big chocolate flavor, it's a relatively guilt-free dessert that will become a standby at all your gatherings. Add fresh strawberries or raspberries and a dollop of sweetened whipped cream if desired.
—Mary Relyea, Canastota, NY

Prep: 20 min. • **Bake:** 40 min. + cooling
Makes: 12 servings

- 1½ cups egg whites (about 10 large)
- 1 cup cake flour
- 2 cups sugar, divided
- ½ cup baking cocoa
- 1 tsp. cream of tartar
- 1 tsp. vanilla extract
- ¼ tsp. salt

GLAZE
- ½ cup semisweet chocolate chips
- 3 Tbsp. half-and-half cream

1. Place the egg whites in a large bowl; let stand at room temperature 30 minutes.
2. Preheat oven to 350°. Sift flour, 1 cup sugar and cocoa together twice.
3. Add cream of tartar, vanilla and salt to egg whites; beat on medium speed until soft peaks form. Gradually add remaining sugar, 2 Tbsp. at a time, beating on high after each addition until the sugar is dissolved. Continue beating until stiff glossy peaks form. Gradually fold in flour mixture, about ½ cup at a time.
4. Gently transfer to an ungreased 10-in. tube pan. Cut through batter with a knife to remove any air pockets. Bake on lowest oven rack until top springs back when lightly touched and cracks feel dry, 40-50 minutes. Immediately invert pan; cool completely in pan, about 1 hour.
5. Run a knife around the sides and the center tube of the pan. Remove cake to a serving plate. For glaze, in a microwave, melt chocolate chips with cream; stir until smooth. Drizzle over cake.

1 slice: 235 cal., 3g fat (2g sat. fat), 2mg chol., 102mg sod., 49g carb. (37g sugars, 1g fiber), 5g pro.

BANANA CREAM PIE

Made from our farm-fresh dairy products, this pretty pie was a sensational, creamy treat anytime Mom served it. Her recipe is a real family treasure. I've never found a version that tastes better!
—Bernice Morris, Marshfield, MO

- -

Prep: 20 min. + cooling • **Makes:** 8 servings

- ¾ cup sugar
- ⅓ cup all-purpose flour
- ¼ tsp. salt
- 2 cups whole milk
- 3 large egg yolks, room temperature, lightly beaten
- 2 Tbsp. butter
- 1 tsp. vanilla extract
- 3 medium, firm bananas
- 1 pastry shell (9 in.), baked
  Optional: Whipped cream and additional sliced bananas

1. In a saucepan, combine sugar, flour and salt; stir in milk and mix well. Cook over medium-high heat until mixture is thickened and bubbly. Cook and stir for 2 minutes longer. Remove from the heat. Stir a small amount into the egg yolks; return all to saucepan. Bring to a gentle boil. Cook and stir 2 minutes; remove from the heat. Add butter and vanilla; cool slightly.
2. Slice the bananas into crust; pour the filling over top. Cool on wire rack for 1 hour. Store in the refrigerator. If desired, before serving, garnish with whipped cream and sliced bananas.

1 slice: 338 cal., 14g fat (7g sat. fat), 101mg chol., 236mg sod., 49g carb. (30g sugars, 1g fiber), 5g pro.

TEST KITCHEN TIP

To ensure a smooth, lump-free filling, stir sugar mixture constantly during cooking, and scrape the sides and bottom of the saucepan with a heatproof rubber spatula.

BANANA CREAM PIE

TILLIE'S GINGER CRUMB CAKE

This recipe goes back at least as far as my grandmother, who was born in the early 1900s. Our sons and I enjoy eating it in a bowl with milk poured on it—much to the dismay of my husband, who prefers it plain!
—Kathy Nienow Clark, Byron, MI

- -

Prep: 20 min. • **Bake:** 35 min.
Makes: 16 servings

- 4 cups all-purpose flour
- 2 cups sugar
- 1 cup cold butter
- ½ tsp. ground ginger
- ¼ tsp. ground cloves
- ½ tsp. ground cinnamon
- ½ tsp. ground nutmeg
- 1 cup plus 2 Tbsp. buttermilk
- 1¼ tsp. baking soda
- 2 large eggs, room temperature

1. In a large bowl, combine flour and sugar; cut in butter until crumbly. Set aside 2 cups. Combine remaining crumb mixture with the remaining ingredients.
2. Sprinkle 1 cup of the reserved crumbs into a greased 12-in. cast-iron skillet or 13x9-in. baking dish. Pour batter over crumbs and sprinkle with remaining crumbs. Bake at 350° until a toothpick inserted in the center comes out clean, about 35 minutes.

1 piece: 330 cal., 13g fat (8g sat. fat), 54mg chol., 232mg sod., 50g carb. (26g sugars, 1g fiber), 5g pro.

GOLDEN
PEACH PIE

¾ cup sour cream
¼ cup 2% milk
2½ cups all-purpose flour
1 tsp. salt
1 tsp. baking powder
½ tsp. baking soda

SYRUP
½ cup sugar
½ cup lemon juice

FROSTING
2 pkg. (8 oz. each) cream cheese, softened
1 cup butter, softened
4 cups confectioners' sugar
1½ tsp. lemon juice
⅛ tsp. salt
Optional: Lemon slices or edible flowers

1. Preheat oven to 350°. Line bottoms of 2 greased 9-in. round baking pans with parchment; grease parchment.
2. Cream butter and sugar until light and fluffy. Add eggs and egg yolks, 1 at a time, beating well after each addition. Beat in lemon zest and juice. In a small bowl, mix sour cream and milk. In another bowl, whisk together the flour, salt, baking powder and baking soda; add to the creamed mixture alternately with sour cream mixture.
3. Transfer to prepared pans. Bake until a toothpick inserted in center comes out clean, 24-28 minutes. Cool in pans for 10 minutes before removing to wire racks; remove parchment. Cool slightly.
4. For the syrup, in a small saucepan, combine sugar and lemon juice. Bring to a boil; cook until the liquid is reduced by half. Cool completely.
5. For frosting, beat the cream cheese and butter until smooth; beat in confectioners' sugar, lemon juice and salt until blended.
6. Using a long serrated knife, cut each cake horizontally in half. Brush layers with warm syrup; cool completely.
7. Place 1 cake layer on a serving plate; spread with 1 cup frosting. Repeat layers twice. Top with remaining cake layer. Frost top and sides with remaining frosting. If desired, top with lemon slices or edible flowers. Refrigerate leftovers.
1 slice: 841 cal., 48g fat (30g sat. fat), 219mg chol., 656mg sod., 96g carb. (72g sugars, 1g fiber), 8g pro.

GOLDEN PEACH PIE

Years ago, I entered this pie in the Park County Fair in Livingston. It won a first-place blue ribbon plus a purple ribbon for Best All Around! Family and friends agree with the judges—it's a perfectly peachy pie.
—Shirley Olson, Polson, MT

- -

Prep: 20 min. • **Bake:** 50 min. + cooling
Makes: 8 servings

2 sheets refrigerated pie crust
5 cups sliced peeled fresh peaches (about 5 medium)
2 tsp. lemon juice
½ tsp. grated orange zest
⅛ tsp. almond extract
1 cup sugar
¼ cup cornstarch
¼ tsp. ground nutmeg
⅛ tsp. salt
2 Tbsp. butter

1. Line a 9-in. pie plate with 1 crust; trim, leaving a 1-in. overhang around edge. Set aside. In a large bowl, combine the peaches, lemon juice, orange zest and almond extract. Combine the sugar, cornstarch, nutmeg and salt. Add to peach mixture; toss gently to coat. Pour into crust; dot with butter.

2. Roll out remaining crust to a ⅛-in.-thick circle; cut into strips of various widths. Arrange over filling in a lattice pattern. Trim and seal strips to bottom crust; fold overhang over. Lightly press or flute edge. Cover the edges loosely with foil.
3. Bake at 400° for 40 minutes. Remove foil; bake until crust is golden brown and filling is bubbly, 10-15 minutes longer. Cool on a wire rack. Store in the refrigerator.
1 piece: 425 cal., 17g fat (8g sat. fat), 18mg chol., 267mg sod., 67g carb. (36g sugars, 2g fiber), 3g pro.

LEMON LAYER CAKE

This citrusy cake with a luscious cream cheese frosting and puckery lemon syrup will garner plenty of raves. The flavor, a duet of sweet and tangy notes, really sings.
—Summer Goddard, Springfield, VA

- -

Prep: 35 min. • **Bake:** 25 min. + cooling
Makes: 12 servings

1 cup butter, softened
1½ cups sugar
2 large eggs, room temperature
3 large egg yolks, room temperature
1 Tbsp. grated lemon zest
2 Tbsp. lemon juice

LEMON LAYER CAKE

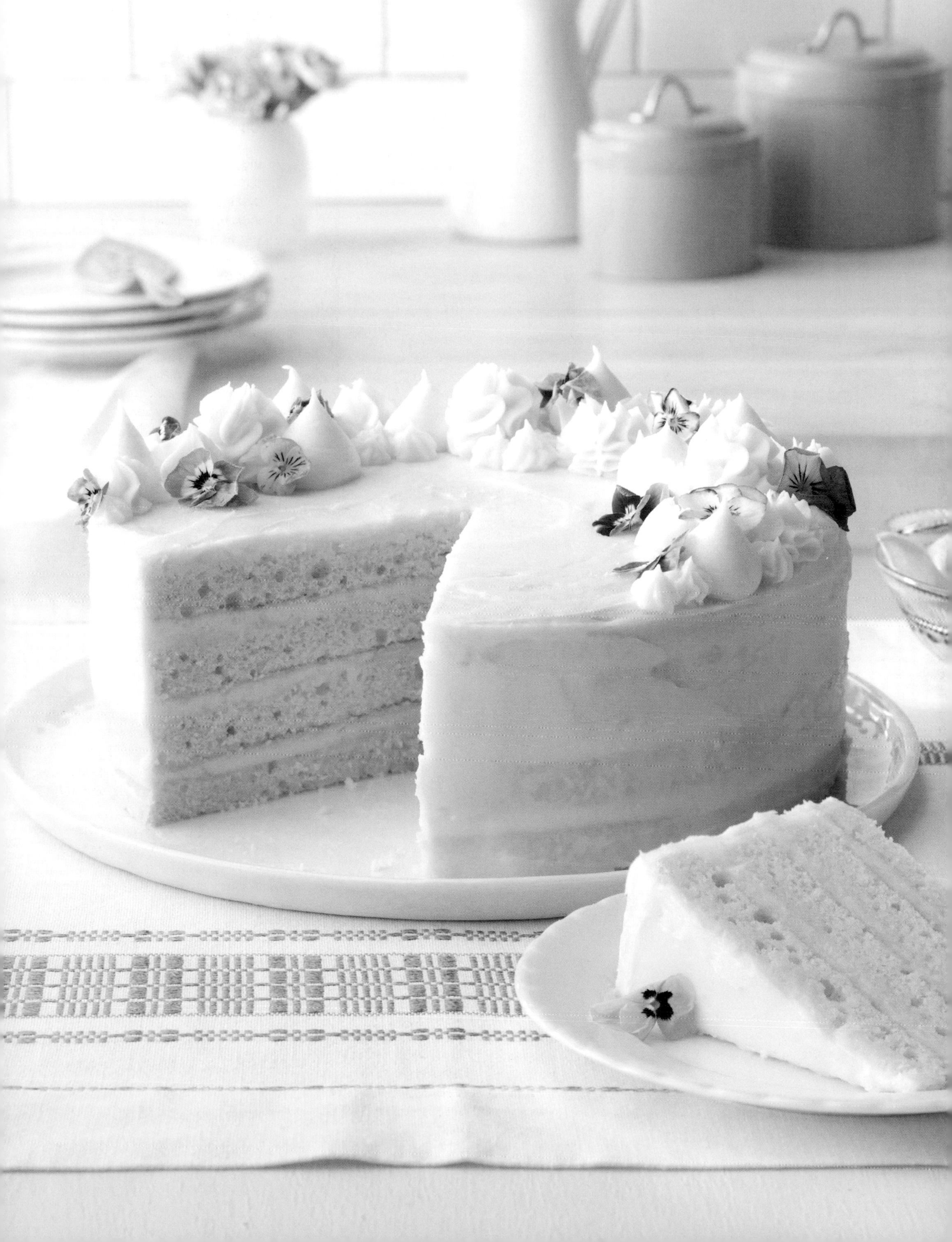

CHERRY PUDDING CAKE

A cross between a cake and a cobbler, this cherry dessert is awesome. Add it to your list of trusty potluck recipes, because this one is sure to go fast.
—Brenda Parker, Kalamazoo, MI

Prep: 10 min. • **Bake:** 40 min.
Makes: 12 servings

    2   cups all-purpose flour
  2½   cups sugar, divided
    4   tsp. baking powder
    1   cup whole milk
    2   Tbsp. canola oil
    2   cans (14½ oz. each) water-packed
        pitted tart red cherries, well drained
    2   to 3 drops red food
        coloring, optional
   ⅛   tsp. almond extract
        Optional: Whipped cream or
        ice cream

1. In a bowl, combine flour, 1 cup of sugar, baking powder, milk and oil; pour into a greased shallow 3-qt. baking dish. In a bowl, combine cherries, food coloring if desired, almond extract and the remaining sugar; spoon over batter.
2. Bake at 375° for 40-45 minutes or until a toothpick inserted in the cake portion comes out clean. Serve warm, if desired with whipped cream or ice cream.
1 serving: 296 cal., 3g fat (1g sat. fat), 3mg chol., 147mg sod., 65g carb. (48g sugars, 1g fiber), 3g pro.

GRANDMA'S SOUR CREAM RAISIN PIE

The aroma of this pie baking in my farm-kitchen oven reminds me of my dear grandma, who made this pretty pie for special occasions.
—Beverly Medalen, Willow City, ND

Prep: 30 min. • **Bake:** 10 min. + chilling
Makes: 8 servings

    1   cup raisins
   ⅔   cup sugar
    3   Tbsp. cornstarch
   ⅛   tsp. salt
   ⅛   tsp. ground cloves
   ½   tsp. ground cinnamon
    1   cup sour cream
   ½   cup whole milk
    3   large egg yolks, room temperature
   ½   cup chopped nuts, optional
    1   pie shell (9 in.), baked
MERINGUE
    3   large egg whites, room temperature
   ¼   tsp. salt
    6   Tbsp. sugar

1. In a small saucepan, place raisins and enough water to cover; bring to a boil. Remove from the heat; set aside.
2. In a large saucepan, combine the sugar, cornstarch, salt, cloves and cinnamon. Stir in sour cream and milk until smooth. Cook and stir over medium-high heat until thickened and bubbly. Reduce heat to low; cook and stir for 2 minutes longer. Remove from the heat. Stir a small amount of hot filling into the egg yolks; return all to the pan, stirring constantly. Bring to a gentle boil; cook and stir 2 minutes. Remove from the heat.
3. Drain the raisins, reserving ½ cup liquid. Gently stir liquid into filling. Add raisins, and nuts if desired. Pour into pie shell.
4. For meringue, in a small bowl, beat egg whites and salt on medium speed until soft peaks form. Gradually beat in the sugar, 1 Tbsp. at a time, on high until stiff peaks form. Spread over the hot filling, sealing the edges to the crust.
5. Bake at 350° for 15 minutes or until golden brown. Cool on a wire rack for 1 hour; refrigerate for 1-2 hours before serving. Refrigerate leftovers.
1 piece: 381 cal., 15g fat (7g sat. fat), 82mg chol., 253mg sod., 58g carb. (40g sugars, 1g fiber), 5g pro.

GRANDMA'S SOUR CREAM RAISIN PIE

**HOLIDAY
HONEY CAKE**

DECADENT FUDGE CAKE

Everyone I serve this to seems to love the rich flavor. Four types of chocolate make it decadent.

—Anna Hogge, Yorktown, VA

Prep: 20 min. • **Bake:** 1¼ hours
Makes: 16 servings

  1   cup butter, softened
1½ cups sugar
  4   large eggs, room temperature
  1   cup buttermilk
  ½   tsp. baking soda
2½ cups all-purpose flour
  8   oz. German sweet chocolate, melted
  1   cup chocolate syrup
  2   tsp. vanilla extract
1¼ cups miniature semisweet
      chocolate chips, divided
  4   oz. white baking chocolate, chopped
  2   Tbsp. plus 1 tsp. shortening, divided

1. Cream butter in a large bowl. Gradually mix in sugar. Add 1 eggs at a time, beating well after each addition. Combine buttermilk and baking soda; add to creamed mixture alternately with flour, beginning and ending with flour. Add melted chocolate, chocolate syrup and vanilla. Stir in 1 cup chocolate chips. Pour the batter into a greased and floured 10-in. fluted tube pan. Bake at 325° for 1¼ hours or until a toothpick comes out clean. Immediately invert cake onto a serving plate; cool completely.
2. Meanwhile, in a microwave, melt white chocolate and 2 Tbsp. shortening; stir until smooth. Cool slightly; drizzle over the cake. Melt remaining chips and shortening in a small saucepan over low heat, stirring until smooth. Remove from the heat; cool slightly. Drizzle over white chocolate.

1 piece: 519 cal., 25g fat (15g sat. fat), 78mg chol., 192mg sod., 63g carb. (44g sugars, 2g fiber), 7g pro.

> *"This nearly put me in a chocolate coma...but I will make it again! Delicious and moist and so chocolaty!"*
> —RENA 55, TASTEOFHOME.COM

HOLIDAY HONEY CAKE

Thirty-five years ago, I gave a friend of mine a platter of assorted home-baked Christmas cookies. The next day, she brought over slices of this delicious cake, which she made for Hanukkah. Naturally, we exchanged recipes, and my family and I have been enjoying this moist and flavorful honey cake ever since! I top my cake with a creamy caramel glaze.

—Kristine Chayes, Smithtown, NY

Prep: 20 min. + standing
Bake: 50 min. + cooling • **Makes:** 12 servings

  3   large eggs, separated
3½ cups all-purpose flour
  1   cup sugar
2½ tsp. baking powder
  1   tsp. baking soda
  1   tsp. ground cinnamon
  ½   tsp. salt
  ½   tsp. ground cloves
  ¼   tsp. ground ginger
1⅓ cups brewed coffee
1⅓ cups honey
  ¼   cup canola oil
  ¼   tsp. cream of tartar
CARAMEL GLAZE
  3   Tbsp. butter
  ⅓   cup packed brown sugar
  2   Tbsp. 2% milk
  ¾   cup confectioners' sugar
  1   tsp. vanilla extract

1. Place egg whites in a large bowl; let stand at room temperature 30 minutes.
2. Meanwhile, preheat oven to 350°. Sift flour, sugar, baking powder, baking soda, cinnamon, salt, cloves and ginger together twice; place in another large bowl.
3. In a small bowl, whisk egg yolks, coffee, honey and oil until smooth. Add to flour mixture; beat until well blended.
4. Add cream of tartar to egg whites; with clean beaters, beat on high speed just until stiff but not dry. Fold a fourth of the whites into batter, then fold in remaining whites.
5. Gently transfer to an ungreased 10-in. tube pan. Bake on lowest oven rack for 50-60 minutes or until top springs back when lightly touched. Immediately invert pan; cool completely, about 1½ hours.
6. In a small heavy saucepan, melt butter. Stir in brown sugar and milk. Bring to a boil; cook over medium heat until sugar is dissolved. Stir in confectioners' sugar and vanilla; cook until thickened, about 5 minutes.
7. Run a knife around sides and center tube of pan. Remove the cake to a serving plate and add the glaze.

1 glazed slice: 452 cal., 9g fat (3g sat. fat), 54mg chol., 350mg sod., 89g carb. (61g sugars, 1g fiber), 6g pro.

GRANDMA'S FAVORITE

DESERTS

From cobblers and creme brulee to tarts and trifles,
old-fashioned desserts always get thumbs-up approval.
Turn here for cheesecakes, frozen treats,
puddings and more, and end your meals
on a sweet note.

OLD-WORLD
RICOTTA
CHEESECAKE

OLD-WORLD RICOTTA CHEESECAKE

I reconstructed this heirloom dessert based on an old recipe that had been in the family for years but was never written down. The subtle cinnamon flavor of the zwieback crust and the dense texture of the ricotta cheese are reminiscent of the cheesecake I enjoyed as a child.
—Mary Beth Jung, Hendersonville, NC

Prep: 20 min. • **Bake:** 1 hour + chilling
Makes: 12 servings

- 1⅔ cups zwieback, rusk or
  plain biscotti crumbs
- 3 Tbsp. sugar
- ½ tsp. ground cinnamon
- ⅓ cup butter, softened

FILLING
- 2 cartons (15 oz. each) ricotta cheese
- ½ cup sugar
- ½ cup half-and-half cream
- 2 Tbsp. all-purpose flour
- 1 Tbsp. lemon juice
- 1 tsp. finely grated lemon zest
- ¼ tsp. salt
- 2 large eggs, room temperature,
  lightly beaten

TOPPING
- 1 cup sour cream
- 2 Tbsp. sugar
- 1 tsp. vanilla extract

1. Combine zwieback crumbs, sugar and cinnamon; mix in butter until mixture is crumbled. Press onto bottom and 1½ in. up sides of a greased 9-in. springform pan. Refrigerate until chilled.
2. Preheat oven to 350°. Beat all the filling ingredients except eggs until smooth. Add eggs; beat on low until combined. Pour into crust. Place pan on a baking sheet.
3. Bake until center is set, about 50 minutes. Remove from oven; let stand 15 minutes, leaving oven on. Combine the topping ingredients; spoon around the edge of the cheesecake. Carefully spread over filling. Bake 10 minutes longer. Loosen sides from pan with a knife; cool 1 hour. Refrigerate for 3 hours or overnight, covering when completely cooled. Remove rim from pan. Refrigerate leftovers.
1 slice: 260 cal., 14g fat (9g sat. fat), 83mg chol., 191mg sod., 25g carb. (16g sugars, 0 fiber), 7g pro.

PEACH & BERRY COBBLER

PEACH & BERRY COBBLER

This is one of my favorite summer recipes, as it features peaches and berries that are in season. But it's just as delicious if you make it with frozen fruit. The quick biscuit topping brings it all together.
—Lauren Knoelke, Des Moines, IA

Prep: 20 min. • **Bake:** 40 min.
Makes: 8 servings

- ½ cup sugar
- 3 Tbsp. cornstarch
- ½ tsp. ground cinnamon
- ¼ tsp. ground cardamom
- 10 medium peaches, peeled
  and sliced (about 6 cups)
- 2 cups mixed blackberries,
  raspberries and blueberries
- 1 Tbsp. lemon juice

TOPPING
- 1 cup all-purpose flour
- ¼ cup sugar
- 2 tsp. grated orange zest
- ¾ tsp. baking powder
- ¼ tsp. salt
- ¼ tsp. baking soda
- 3 Tbsp. cold butter
- ¾ cup buttermilk
  Vanilla ice cream, optional

1. Preheat oven to 375°. In a large bowl, mix sugar, cornstarch, cinnamon and cardamom. Add peaches, berries and lemon juice; toss to combine. Transfer to a 10-in. cast-iron or other ovenproof skillet.
2. In a small bowl, whisk the first 6 topping ingredients; cut in butter until the mixture resembles coarse crumbs. Add buttermilk; stir just until moistened. Drop mixture by tablespoonfuls over peach mixture.
3. Bake, uncovered, until topping is golden brown, 40-45 minutes. Serve warm. If desired, top with vanilla ice cream.
1 serving: 279 cal., 5g fat (3g sat. fat), 12mg chol., 238mg sod., 57g carb. (38g sugars, 5g fiber), 4g pro.

GRANDMA'S ENGLISH TRIFLE

This delicious recipe was my grandmother's. I remember Mother telling me stories from her girlhood—especially how her mother would make an enormous dish of this for Saturday night dinners, when they often had guests. If there were leftovers, they'd have that trifle for dessert every night that week until it was gone! Nowadays, on our dairy farm, this recipe always goes over big with my husband and our six children.
—Ruth Verratti, Gasport, NY

- -

Prep: 30 min. + chilling • **Makes:** 10 servings

1   prepared loaf pound cake or 1 pkg. (10¾ oz.) frozen pound cake, thawed
¼   to ½ cup raspberry jam
1   pkg. (3 to 3½ oz.) regular or instant vanilla pudding mix
2½ cups 2% milk
1   cup chilled heavy whipping cream
3   Tbsp. confectioners' sugar
    Slivered almonds
    Maraschino cherries, halved

Slice pound cake in half horizontally. Spread with jam and replace top of cake. Slice cake into 9 pieces. Line the sides and fill the center of a 2-qt. glass serving bowl with cake pieces. Prepare pudding with milk. Pour over cake. Chill. Beat cream and sugar until soft peaks form; spread over cake and pudding. Chill at least 4 hours. Garnish with slivered almonds and cherries.

1 serving: 292 cal., 16g fat (10g sat. fat), 76mg chol., 176mg sod., 31g carb. (24g sugars, 0 fiber), 4g pro.

BANANA BREAD PUDDING

BANANA BREAD PUDDING

With its crusty golden top, custard-like inside and smooth vanilla sauce, this bread pudding from my grandmother is a real homespun dessert. I enjoy making it for my grandchildren.
—Mary Detweiler, Middlefield, OH

- -

Prep: 10 min. • **Bake:** 40 min.
Makes: 6 servings

4   cups cubed day-old French or sourdough bread (1-in. pieces)
¼   cup butter, melted
3   large eggs
2   cups whole milk
½   cup sugar
2   tsp. vanilla extract
½   tsp. ground cinnamon
½   tsp. ground nutmeg
½   tsp. salt
1   cup sliced firm bananas (¼-in. pieces)
SAUCE
3   Tbsp. butter
2   Tbsp. sugar
1   Tbsp. cornstarch
¾   cup whole milk
¼   cup light corn syrup
1   tsp. vanilla extract

1. Place the bread cubes in a greased 2-qt. casserole; pour butter over top and toss to coat. In a medium bowl, lightly beat eggs; add milk, sugar, vanilla, cinnamon, nutmeg and salt. Stir in bananas.
2. Pour over the bread cubes and stir to coat. Bake, uncovered, at 375° for about 40 minutes or until a knife inserted in the center comes out clean.
3. Meanwhile, for sauce, melt butter in a small saucepan. Combine the sugar and cornstarch; add to butter. Stir in milk and corn syrup. Cook and stir over medium heat until the mixture comes to a full boil. Boil for 1 minute. Remove from the heat; stir in the vanilla. Serve warm sauce over warm pudding.

1 piece: 439 cal., 21g fat (12g sat. fat), 157mg chol., 561mg sod., 56g carb. (38g sugars, 1g fiber), 9g pro.

TURTLE PRALINE TART

This decadent dessert is my own creation, and I'm very proud of it. It's easy enough to make for everyday meals but special enough to serve guests or take to a potluck.
—Kathy Specht, Clinton, MT

Prep: 35 min. + chilling • **Makes:** 16 servings

1	sheet refrigerated pie crust
36	caramels
1	cup heavy whipping cream, divided
3½	cups pecan halves
½	cup semisweet chocolate chips, melted

1. Preheat oven to 450°. Unroll the pie crust on a lightly floured surface. Transfer to an 11-in. fluted tart pan with removable bottom; trim edges.
2. Line unpricked pie crust with a double thickness of heavy-duty foil. Bake 8 minutes. Remove foil; bake until light golden brown, 5-6 minutes longer. Cool on a wire rack.
3. In a large saucepan, combine caramels and ½ cup heavy whipping cream. Cook and stir over medium-low heat until caramels are melted. Stir in pecans. Spread filling evenly into crust. Drizzle with melted chocolate.
4. Refrigerate until set, about 30 minutes. Whip remaining cream; serve with tart.
1 slice: 335 cal., 24g fat (4g sat. fat), 4mg chol., 106mg sod., 31g carb. (19g sugars, 3g fiber), 4g pro.

TURTLE PRALINE TART

MUST-HAVE TIRAMISU

This is the perfect guilt-free version of a classic dessert. My friends and family even say that they prefer my lighter recipe over traditional tiramisu.
—Ale Gambini, Beverly Hills, CA

Prep: 25 min. + chilling • **Makes:** 9 servings

½	cup heavy whipping cream
2	cups vanilla yogurt
1	cup fat-free milk
½	cup brewed espresso or strong coffee, cooled
24	crisp ladyfinger cookies
	Baking cocoa
	Fresh raspberries, optional

1. In a small bowl, beat cream until stiff peaks form; fold in yogurt. Spread ½ cup cream mixture onto bottom of an 8-in. square dish.
2. In a shallow dish, mix milk and espresso. Quickly dip 12 ladyfinger cookies into coffee mixture, allowing excess to drip off. Arrange in dish in a single layer, breaking to fit as needed. Top with half of the remaining cream mixture; dust with baking cocoa. Repeat layers.
3. Refrigerate tiramisu, covered, at least 2 hours before serving. If desired, serve with fresh raspberries.
1 piece: 177 cal., 6g fat (4g sat. fat), 41mg chol., 80mg sod., 25g carb. (18g sugars, 0 fiber), 6g pro. **Diabetic exchanges:** 1 starch, ½ fat-free milk, 1 fat.

CARAMEL CREME BRULEE

CHOCOLATE TART WITH CRANBERRY RASPBERRY SAUCE

A little of this tart goes a long way, with its rich chocolate and fruit flavors. If you want to make this dessert even more special, top it with whipped cream!
—Diane Nemitz, Ludington, MI

- -

Prep: 40 min. • **Bake:** 40 min. + cooling
Makes: 12 servings

- 1   cup all-purpose flour
- ½   cup old-fashioned oats
- ¼   cup sugar
- ½   cup cold butter, cubed
- 1½ cups unblanched almonds
- ½   cup packed brown sugar
- ½   cup dark corn syrup
- 2   large eggs
- 4   oz. bittersweet chocolate, melted
- 2   Tbsp. butter, melted

SAUCE
- 2   cups fresh raspberries, divided
- 1   cup fresh or frozen cranberries, thawed
- ¾   cup sugar
- 2   Tbsp. port wine or water

1. Preheat oven to 350°. Process the flour, oats and sugar in a food processor until the oats are ground. Add the butter; pulse until crumbly. Press onto the bottom and 1 in. up sides of an ungreased 10-in. springform pan. Bake until lightly browned, 14-16 minutes. Cool on a wire rack.
2. Process almonds in a food processor until coarsely chopped. Beat brown sugar, corn syrup, eggs, chocolate and melted butter; stir in almonds.
3. Pour into prepared crust. Bake until the center is set and the crust is golden brown, 25-30 minutes. Cool the tart completely on a wire rack.
4. Meanwhile, in a small saucepan, combine 1 cup raspberries, cranberries, sugar and wine. Bring to a boil, stirring to dissolve the sugar. Reduce heat to low; cook, uncovered, until cranberries pop, 4-5 minutes, stirring occasionally. Remove mixture from heat; cool slightly.
5. Press the berry mixture through a fine-mesh strainer into a bowl; discard seeds. Refrigerate sauce until serving.
6. Remove rim from pan. Serve tart with sauce and remaining raspberries.
1 slice with 4 tsp. sauce: 462 cal., 24 fat (9g sat. fat), 56mg chol., 115mg sod., 55g carb. (39g sugars, 4g fiber), 7g pro.

CARAMEL CREME BRULEE

This recipe comes out perfect every time and it's always a crowd pleaser! A torch works best to get the sugar caramelized while keeping the rest of the custard cool. You may want to use even more sugar to create a thicker, more even crust on top.
—Jenna Fleming, Lowville, NY

- -

Prep: 20 min. • **Bake:** 40 min. + chilling
Makes: 14 servings

- 4½ cups heavy whipping cream
- 1½ cups half-and-half cream
- 15 large egg yolks
- 1⅓ cups sugar, divided
- 3   tsp. caramel extract
- ¼   tsp. salt
- ⅓   cup packed brown sugar

1. Preheat oven to 325°. In a large saucepan, heat the whipping cream and cream until bubbles form around sides of pan; remove from heat. In a bowl, whisk egg yolks, 1 cup sugar, extract and salt until blended but not foamy. Slowly stir in the hot cream mixture.
2. Place an ungreased broiler-safe 13x9-in. baking dish in a baking pan large enough to hold it without touching the sides. Pour the egg mixture into dish. Place pan on oven rack; add very hot water to pan to within 1 in. of top of dish. Bake 40-50 minutes or until the center is just set and top appears dull. Immediately remove the dish from the water bath to a wire rack; cool 1 hour. Refrigerate until cold.
3. Mix brown sugar and remaining sugar. To caramelize topping with a kitchen torch, sprinkle custard evenly with sugar mixture. Hold torch flame about 2 in. above custard surface and rotate it slowly until sugar is evenly caramelized. Serve immediately or refrigerate up to 1 hour.
4. To caramelize the topping in a broiler, let custard stand at room temperature for 30 minutes. Preheat broiler. Sprinkle custard evenly with sugar mixture. Broil 3-4 in. from heat until sugar is caramelized, 2-3 minutes. Serve custard immediately or refrigerate for up to 1 hour.
NOTE: This recipe was tested with Watkin's caramel extract.
½ cup: 452 cal., 35g fat (21g sat. fat), 298mg chol., 86mg sod., 28g carb. (27g sugars, 0 fiber), 6g pro.

CHOCOLATE TART
WITH CRANBERRY
RASPBERRY SAUCE

CHOCOLATE BAVARIAN TORTE

Whenever I take this torte to a potluck, I get so many requests for the recipe.
—Edith Holmstrom, Madison, WI

Prep: 15 min. + chilling
Bake: 30 min. + cooling
Makes: 12 servings

- 1 pkg. devil's food cake mix (regular size)
- 1 pkg. (8 oz.) cream cheese, softened
- ⅓ cup packed brown sugar
- 1 tsp. vanilla extract
- ⅛ tsp. salt
- 2 cups heavy whipping cream, whipped
- 2 Tbsp. grated semisweet chocolate

1. Prepare and bake the devil's food cake according to package directions, using two 9-in. round baking pans. Cool in pans for 10 minutes before removing to wire racks to cool completely.
2. In a large bowl, beat cream cheese, sugar, vanilla and salt until smooth. Fold in cream.
3. Cut each cake horizontally into 2 layers. Place bottom layer on a serving plate; top with a fourth of the cream mixture. Sprinkle with a fourth of the chocolate. Repeat the layers 3 times. Cover and refrigerate torte for 8 hours or overnight.
1 piece: 495 cal., 33g fat (16g sat. fat), 111mg chol., 475mg sod., 45g carb. (27g sugars, 1g fiber), 6g pro.

MAMA'S BLACKBERRY COBBLER

Alabama has some tasty fresh blackberries. Decades ago my mama was going to pick blackberries to make a cobbler, but she went to the hospital to have me instead. This is her mama's recipe.
—Lisa Allen, Joppa, AL

Prep: 15 min. • **Bake:** 45 min.
Makes: 6 servings

- ½ cup plus 2 Tbsp. melted butter, divided
- 1 cup self-rising flour
- 1½ cups sugar, divided
- 1 cup 2% milk
- ½ tsp. vanilla extract
- 3 cups fresh blackberries or frozen unsweetened blackberries

1. Preheat oven to 350°. Pour ½ cup melted butter into an 8-in. square baking dish. In a small bowl, combine flour, 1 cup sugar, milk and vanilla extract until blended; pour into prepared dish. In another bowl, combine blackberries, remaining ½ cup sugar and remaining 2 Tbsp. melted butter; toss until combined. Spoon over batter.
2. Bake until topping is golden brown and fruit is tender, 45-50 minutes. Serve warm.
¾ cup: 491 cal., 21g fat (13g sat. fat), 54mg chol., 421mg sod., 75g carb. (56g sugars, 4g fiber), 5g pro.

> ### TEST KITCHEN TIP
> Be sure to disperse the berry mixture evenly and all the way to the edges of the dish.

CHOCOLATE BAVARIAN TORTE

HOMEMADE STRAWBERRY ICE CREAM

What could be better than a tubful of luscious homemade ice cream made with fresh strawberries? Having an ice cream social at church with more of the same!
—Esther Johnson, Merrill, WI

- -

Prep: 20 min. + cooling
Process: 20 min./batch + freezing
Makes: 12 servings (about 1½ qt.)

    6 large egg yolks
    2 cups whole milk
    1 cup sugar
    ¼ tsp. salt
    1 tsp. vanilla extract
    2 cups heavy whipping cream
    2 cups crushed fresh
       strawberries, sweetened

1. Place egg yolks and milk in the top of a double boiler; beat. Add sugar and salt. Cook over simmering water, stirring until mixture is thickened and coats a metal spoon. Cool.
2. Add vanilla extract, cream and crushed strawberries. Pour into the cylinder of an ice cream freezer and freeze according to manufacturer's directions. When ice cream is frozen, transfer to a freezer container; freeze for 2-4 hours before serving.
½ cup: 265 cal., 19g fat (11g sat. fat), 166mg chol., 88mg sod., 22g carb. (21g sugars, 1g fiber), 4g pro.

STRAWBERRY
PRETZEL DESSERT

STRAWBERRY PRETZEL DESSERT

A salty pretzel crust nicely contrasts with the sweet cream cheese and gelatin layers.
—Aldene Belch, Flint, MI

- -

Prep: 20 min. • **Bake:** 10 min. + chilling
Makes: 16 servings

    2 cups crushed pretzels (about 8 oz.)
    ¾ cup butter, melted
    3 Tbsp. sugar
FILLING
    2 cups whipped topping
    1 pkg. (8 oz.) cream cheese, softened
    1 cup sugar
TOPPING
    2 pkg. (3 oz. each) strawberry gelatin
    2 cups boiling water
    2 pkg. (16 oz. each) frozen sweetened
       sliced strawberries, thawed
       Optional: Additional whipped
       topping and pretzels

1. In a bowl, combine the pretzels, butter and sugar. Press into an ungreased 13x9-in. baking dish. Bake at 350° for 10 minutes. Cool on a wire rack.
2. For filling, in a small bowl, beat whipped topping, cream cheese and sugar until smooth. Spread over the pretzel crust. Refrigerate until chilled.
3. For topping, dissolve the gelatin in boiling water in a large bowl. Stir in the sweetened strawberries; chill until partially set. Carefully spoon over filling. Chill until firm, 4-6 hours. Cut into squares; serve with additional whipped topping and pretzels if desired.
1 piece: 295 cal., 15g fat (10g sat. fat), 39mg chol., 305mg sod., 38g carb. (27g sugars, 1g fiber), 3g pro.

RECIPE INDEX